PA Guide to

Export

Second Edition

Peter Newson and
Jason Craig

THE **PUBLISHERS**
ASSOCIATION

First published as *Guide to Export for UK Book Publishers*, Barney Allan
Financed by UK Trade & Investment (c) The Publishers Association 2004
Second edition published 2011 Peter Newsom and Jason Craig
© The Publishers Association 2011

The Publishers Association
29B Montague Street
London
WC1B 5BW
t +44 (0)207 691 9191
f +44(0) 207 691 9199
e mail@publishers.org.uk
w www.publishers.org.uk

ISBN: 978-0-85386-358-8

Front cover globe graphic:© Fotolia.com/ktsdesign
All other graphics unless otherwise indicated, sourced from istockphoto.com and fotolia.com
Printed and bound in the UK by Lightning Source UK Ltd, Milton Keynes, Buckinghamshire

Contents

Foreword

Welcome to this second edition of the *PA Guide to Export*. The first edition of this immensely popular guide was published in 2004 with the support of UK Trade & Investment and authored by Barney Allen. We are delighted to have Peter Newsom, most recently Export Sales Director at Headline and now consulting on export sales strategy to a range of UK publishers as author of this updated edition. Thanks also go to  Jason Craig, Penguin UK Group Digital Sales Director who has written a completely new section (Section 4) on the Export of Digital Products.

The most recent PA statistics released at the beginning of May 2011 (and published in the *PA Statistics Yearbook 2010*[1]) demonstrates the increasing importance of export markets for the UK's physical books. With a year-on-year increase of 4 per cent in 2010 (by value), export sales now account for 40 per cent of total sales, equating to £1.25 billion. Key export markets are still the USA, Ireland, Germany, Netherlands, Australia, Singapore and Canada, but it should be noted that Europe as a region accounts for 37 per cent of total exports proving that sales opportunities for the new exporter are within easy reach.

The new challenge facing the exporter is indeed how we export our ebooks, and the new section in this revised edition will deal with how you approach your ebook strategy for export markets. It is clear that marketing and connecting with our consumers will be a key activity for selling ebooks. It will also be vital to keep established export customers up to date on how to access digital content for sales to consumers. These export customers will need to understand the new opportunities open to them and be able to supply content to the consumer in any way demanded in order to remain relevant.

---

1   The export figures from the *PA Statistics Yearbook 2010* can be found in Appendix 1 of this guide.

We will be watching with interest to see how export sales statistics and strategies evolve and change with the impact, or perhaps even cannibalisation, from both sales of ebooks and online sales of physical books internationally. Measuring and evaluating these new and constantly changing supply chains will be an important but testing task for future consideration.

In the meantime, export of physical books remains a core activity and will continue to do so for a long time. Having an export strategy is the key to success. This guide is designed to assist with the whole process from setting up and managing your supply chain, product management for export and the important role of credit control. It also includes a list of useful contacts to help you on your way.

My personal thanks go to UKTI for all their support for our sector and to PA members who sit on our international board and working parties and who share their wealth of knowledge and experience; contributing to improving conditions in our export markets for everyone.

Emma House
Trade and International Director

The authors

Peter Newsom is an international sales consultant and a former International Sales Director with over 30 years experience in global markets. In 2010, Peter co-authored the *PA Guide to International Book Fairs* with Gloria Bailey and Lynette Owen.

Jason Craig is Penguin UK's Group Digital Sales Director, with responsibility for Penguin UK's digital sales in all territories for which they hold rights. He has spent twenty years working in publishing across New Zealand, Australia and for the last ten years here in the UK. His digital experience started in covering online accounts (including Amazon) for Penguin from 2003, and in 2008 was one of the core PUK team tasked with transitioning the business to a digital future.

Introduction

UK publishers have traditionally relied on export sales for a large part of their revenue. For example, academic publishers can sell as much as 70 per cent of their output in overseas markets, and for trade publishers it is as much as 40 per cent.

The continuing globalisation of the world book market, and the unstoppable progress of English as a world language, mean that addressing international markets is becoming more important than ever. There are currently around 400 million 'native' speakers of English world-wide, and English has become the dominant or in some instances the required language of aviation, communications, information technology, science, entertainment and diplomacy. Up to 1.4 billion people worldwide use English as a second language and it is anticipated that a further 2 billion will be learning English during the next decade. The phenomenon, therefore, of this growing global population of English-speakers represents an outstanding opportunity for the UK publishing community to increase their international sales. Cheaper transport costs and telephone calls, and the benefits of email and the internet combine to make exporting books easier than ever before.

Selling foreign and English-language rights to overseas publishers is often the first step made by UK houses in the international market. Rights sales can be a useful source of income for small and medium-sized publishers; illustrated publishers traditionally depend on pre-selling a US or foreign-language co-edition to fund their print runs, and smaller academic publishers can generate useful cash flow by selling editions to American university presses and others. Co-editions in particular allow you to build your print run and so reduce costs on your own edition. Foreign-language rights sales also keep authors happy, and can generate good income if the numbers of either the foreign-language print run, or copies sold, is big enough.

However, rights sales can be of limited benefit and effectiveness as a total export strategy, for the following reasons:

- *Risk of leakage:* This applies only to English-language rights sales, but the edition you sell to a US or Indian publisher can easily find its way back into your home or export markets via today's globalised book-supply chain.

- *Skimming:* Rights buyers tend to focus on your best product only, leaving your backlist and midlist titles hung out to dry.

- *Cost versus benefits:* Selling rights can be expensive in terms of time and travel, and can offer only limited returns. In the case of foreign-language rights, much of the revenue tends to be eaten up by agents' fees, taxes, and the author's share.

- *The invisible brand:* Selling English-language or foreign rights in particular does nothing to build trade and consumer awareness of your brand. The credit for publishing your great title will be taken by the local publisher.

- *Revenue:* Ultimately, selling your own editions offers you more revenue and margin than rights sales.

- *Market development:* Selling rights does not allow you to interact with, and learn from, your overseas markets in the same way that selling copies does.

Establishing an effective sales, marketing and distribution operation for export sales can complement rights sales, and even enhance them. The more you know about your export markets, the more likely you are to sell both. By selling your own stock overseas you can make virtues of all the downsides of selling rights.

1 Approaching export markets

1.1 Is it worth it?

Setting out an export sales plan, and executing it successfully, is a challenge for many small and medium-sized publishers. The time and expense involved in attending Frankfurt Book Fair alone – the starting point for many publishers' international ventures – is considerable. For small publishers in particular, the prime focus is the home market, which is familiar, highly  centralised, and easy to access. Export markets present a bewildering array of opportunities and challenges, not all of which are immediately apparent, and many of which seem to offer small rewards compared with those on offer in the UK. So why should publishers bother with an export plan? The answer is that it really is worth it!

1.2 The benefits of export

1.2.1 Market size

The total annual value of the export market for books in English is estimated at around £3.0 billion (based on customs and excise figures), which is split between UK and US companies. Publishing phenomena such as the Harry Potter series, Stephanie Meyer's crossover novels, Dan Brown, or Stieg Larsson's Millenium Trilogy have sold either as many copies or more in export markets as they have in the UK. The German market for UK publishers is alone worth £137m. Even the poorest countries can yield sales for publishers, because they benefit from World Bank and other aid-funded book-buying projects worth tens of millions of pounds every year.

1.2.2 More sales and profits

Exporting offers your business increased volume and margins. For example, book buyers in Europe and South East Asia offer tremendous value as customers for academic product, because they can sell large volumes and will accept relatively modest discounts, and in the same areas terms for trade books are comparable to many of those in the UK but benefit from much lower royalty rates

1.2.3 Incremental sales

Even in relatively low-margin markets like South Asia or Africa, sales of quantities at high discount offer the benefits of increased print runs, lowering unit costs across your whole run.

1.2.4 Spread market risk and opportunity

Extending the range of markets in which you operate gives you more options for spreading risk; growth in export markets can help make up for lean years in the home market.

1.2.5 Attract and retain authors

Most authors are very excited at the prospect of their book being sold in Oslo or Taipei. A strong export capability is a good way of attracting and keeping the best authors.

1.2.6 New publishing opportunities

An active export sales and marketing programme can open up whole new worlds of publishing opportunity. In the case of one small business publisher, fast work in partnership with their distributor in South East Asia helped to net sales of 8,000 copies of a book on the Asian economic crash of 1997. Academic reference publishers have traditionally worked closely with Japanese retailers and wholesalers to sell quantities of high-priced reprint sets to libraries.

1.2.7 Build the value of your business

Having a functioning export sales capability increases your frontlist and backlist sales across the whole list, and builds the value of your business in the eyes of any potential investors or purchasers.

1.2.8 Motivate staff

There is an export 'feelgood' factor deriving from the excitement (and sometimes even drama) of export: overseas travel, meeting and befriending international customers, and opening up new markets spreads a sense of success and growth throughout your company. Overseas customers can be demanding, and even exasperating, but getting to know them is a fascinating process, and can be fun.

1.2.9 Raise your profile

Building an international market presence raises the profile of your brand world-wide, increasing even domestic buyers' awareness of your brand, and confidence in your products.

1.2.10 It has never been easier

You do not have to speak 14 foreign languages to navigate your way to export markets and meet international customers, the vast majority of whom can do business with you in English. Cheap air fares, the revolution of email and the internet, and the global march of English as the world's language all add up to a tremendous opportunity – right here, right now.

1.3 Planning for market entry

Successful export campaigns require good planning. Planning involves researching your market, making financial forecasts of costs, and projections of likely sales.

The planning process can be guided by the *IDIC Model* developed by US marketing gurus Don Peppers and Martha Rogers:

- *Identify* the size and shape of market opportunity.
- *Differentiate* both your priority and your target markets.
- *Interact* with your export agents, distributors and retailers.
- *Customise* your product offer and promotion strategy according to market needs.

1.3.1 Forewarned is forearmed

Publishers committing to an export strategy need to be aware of the costs and risks of market entry. Embarking on an export strategy involves the commitment of management time, and the allocation of human and financial resources. It may require you to hire new staff, or to commit to distribution deals that involve the consignment of stock that may turn into a costly write-off. You may also find yourself dealing in unfamiliar legal and regulatory environments. There is also a credit risk, in that your export customers may prove unwilling or unable to pay you. Or, more likely, they may just pay you very slowly, resulting in cash flow problems for your business.

1.3.2 Set priorities by market

The main criteria for prioritising markets are market size, profitability, creditworthiness, and ease of access. North America, Australia and New Zealand, Europe and the richer Asian countries are the best places to start. Bear in mind that markets with one or two key distributors or retail chains will enable you to get quite broad coverage via a single point of entry.

1.3.3 Research the markets

- *What is the market size in your sector?* Market sizing for English-language books overseas is an inexact art because of the many channels used to access the markets, but you can usually estimate the sales potential for your list by combining research from the PA's website and other sources.

- *What are the main routes to market? Who are the major players?* You need to identify the agents, distributors, retailers, and mail-order specialists in your field. These may be retailers, library suppliers, wholesalers, or even non-book companies. There are also UK-based wholesalers and library suppliers who export books.

- *What are the prevailing discounts and credit terms?* Generally, export credit terms are more generous than in the UK, to take account of the longer supply chain. Discounts can be higher than in the UK, although not in all cases. If you are selling scientific, technical and medical (STM) products into Japan, you can expect to offer relatively low discounts, while to sell mass-market paperbacks to a wholesaler in India, you will need to offer either ultra high discounts or net prices based on unit cost and royalty plus a wafer thin margin.

- *What returns allowance, if any, do the customers expect?* In many export markets firm sale is the norm, although some may expect a small credit now and again to compensate for dead stock. To sell to Europe's leading trade distributors, full returns rights are often demanded though reasonable percentages can usually be negotiated.

- *Is censorship an issue?* Religion, politics, and dietary taboos are the likeliest cause of problems and even mildly sexual content is very tricky to sell in some Middle Eastern countries. Harry Potter was banned in some conservative Christian markets in Europe because it was deemed to be promoting witchcraft. Map and atlas publishers have to be on their guard about how they tackle disputed borders and territories. One ELT publisher lost a textbook adoption in Saudi Arabia because their cover featured the spar of a yacht, which the censors interpreted as a sneaky attempt to evangelise with an image of the Christian cross. Be prepared to submit samples for censorship in advance, where appropriate.

- *What promotional materials are required?* In most cases, UK catalogues and leaflets can be used, but these may need adapting or customising to suit local needs. In particular, your catalogues should feature very clear contact information for your sales and marketing, distribution and credit control people and telephone numbers should quote the accepted international forms, e.g., London numbers should appear as +44 (0)20 1234 5678.

- *Are there any book fairs that can be used to launch your export drive?* Frankfurt, London and Book Expo America are good places to meet export customers. There are also regional and national fairs that you can attend, although some are little more than local book bazaars. The best of them, such as Bologna for children's books, Beijing, Abu Dhabi, and even Taipei provide good opportunities to meet your potential customers and start selling books.

- *Are you prepared to offer exclusivity?* This is often the first request of export customers, and you should be ready for it. Exclusivity for either your whole list or particular product lines can be a good way of opening up a market as it justifies your customer's promotion efforts and consolidates your business into one convenient channel. As your export selling campaign matures, you may find that exclusive arrangements can limit your growth and create ill-feeling among other retailers who may not be happy to buy from your exclusive local source. Remember too that customers now have many ways to 'buy round' any arrangement you make. Parallel imports are commonly made via wholesalers in the UK and USA. Ultimately, experience in the market and asking around other publishers will be your best guide as to when to go exclusive and when to keep markets open.

1.4   Sources of information

Sources of information on export markets include the following:

1.4.1   Publishers' catalogues

It is worth checking the catalogues and websites of other publishers in your segment to see which agents and distributors they are using.

1.4.2   Agents and book importers

It may seem rather a truism, but the best source of current information on export markets is overseas representatives and agents and book importing customers in key markets.

1.4.3   Consultants

The publishing industry regularly sheds experienced international sales and marketing people, many of whom set up consultancy services that can offer you a short cut to the market know-how you need.

1.4.4   The Publishers Association

The PA's website (www.publishers.org.uk) is useful for accessing market reports on more than 50 countries, including contact details for booksellers and agents, information on market sizes, and other data. Recent major country reports cover Japan, Taiwan, Russia, and South Africa. The PA site also features useful information on international book fairs, grants available for exhibitors and, in the international section, information about outward delegations.

1.4.5   Local trade associations

Local trade associations and book chambers can be useful sources of information about current conditions in local markets. For contact details visit the websites of the International Publishers Association and the regional trade associations such as the Federation of European Publishers as they provide links to their members (see Appendix 7).

1.4.6   Export sales managers

Export sales managers of major companies can usually be very helpful – most will be happy to share advice and their knowledge of the market with you. Many big publishers represent third-party publishers in export markets, and so have experience of the challenges and opportunities facing small and medium-sized houses.

1.4.7   Trade delegations

The PA organises approximately one to two outward trade delegations a year on a self-funding basis. Participation can be a cost effective and worthwhile means of familiarising and researching an unknown market through face-to-face meetings.

The benefits of participating in such a delegation include:

- the opportunity to visit customers and potential customers.
- the fact that local booksellers and importers can feel more secure in dealing with new companies that they meet via an official or semi-official mission.
- meetings with librarians, academics, and government officials (most of whom may not be so accessible to individual publishers).
- the usefulness of being in the market with the representatives of other houses.
- collective briefings with information about terms, currency exchange and other essentials which can otherwise be relatively hard to come by.
- an opportunity to identify potential agents/representatives.
- frequently supported by the local embassy or High Commission.

Further details of proposed PA outward delegations can be found on the PA's website (www.publishers.org.uk/events).

1.4.8 UK Trade & Investment

UK Trade & Investment (www.ukti.gov.uk) is the government department that helps UK-based companies succeed in the global economy. UKTI offers specialist guidance, overseas market reports and sales leads. As well as assistance to visit overseas markets and exhibit at key international events. For further information see Appendix 11.

1.5 Export marketing strategy: setting priorities

Having researched your market, you will have built up a clearer picture of your priorities in terms of both product lines and broad market areas. Your next steps should include investigating the following:

- *Market value:* volume, margin and growth potential.
- *Market characteristics:* economic, demographic, use of English, educational system, trade network, access, key buying seasons.
- *Key customers:* retailers, wholesalers, chains.
- *Agency/distributor options:* offshore and onshore.
- *UK-based exporting suppliers:* for example, library suppliers and wholesalers (the latter are increasingly important in Europe).
- *Key product for the market:* differentiate your international bestsellers-to-be.
- *Resource allocation:* trips, marketing spend, commissions, incentives.
- *Expectations*: sales forecasts and cost of sales projections.

1.6 General principles for approaching export markets

1.6.1 Be realistic

The first priority is to *be realistic* about your prospects, and the real potential for your list. This will save you time and ensure that you are not disappointed. Do not expect miracles in export if you are publishing books on Waterways of Worcestershire or The X Factor. Similarly, understand that you will have to accept local price points if you want to enter the market – even though these can seem very low (for example, in India or the Philippines), and you may not be able to make them work for you.

1.6.2 Profile your list

Profile your list clearly. In a document to accompany your catalogue, describe your list, its main strengths, and where it sells in other markets. Make comparisons with better-known publishers where you have analogous product. Using clear, straightforward language, your company profile should include:

- An overview of your company.
- Selling points strengths, bestselling titles, reviews if appropriate.
- Competition.
- Marketing support and schedule of catalogues.
- General (and very conservative) information on discounts and terms of trade.
- Broad-brush turnover figures for sales in the UK and export.
- Bestseller lists for both UK and export markets.

1.7 Issues for export

1.7.1 Prioritise

Prioritise the best and richest markets. These may depend on your product sector. For example, for trade product Europe, Australia and ASEAN (Singapore, Malaysia, Thailand, Indonesia, the Philippines) may be the most worthwhile markets, but for academic or STM the focus should include Northern Europe and Asian markets such as Japan, Korea and Taiwan, which all have relatively rich library markets served by efficient local importers.

1.7.2 Make resources available

Make resources available for addressing the market – this may be time or money for mailing, travel, etc. Probably most important is to have at least some time from a junior to mid-level marketing executive to provide 'sales service' to the markets. This includes promotional support, such as mailing and organising book fair participation, as well as customer service support to sort out queries. It will also be worthwhile spending some time training your distributor's customer service people, and even hiring foreign-language speakers if you can.

1.7.3 Allocate resources and build partnerships

Whichever method or level of interaction with the market you decide on, the key to success is *allocating resources* to develop sales (especially a travel and entertaining budget for foreign trips and book fairs), as well as a back office 'sales service' support). Now you can focus on selecting the *best partners* for your international sales effort, and building the *best possible relationships* with the key players for your list in the market.

1.7.4 Management

International sales management can be a high-maintenance task. Agents, distributors and customers need constant servicing of their orders, requests for promotional support, complaints and queries. They also need encouraging, driving and chasing to maintain their sales efforts.

1.7.5 Editorial direction

A major factor in deciding the sales and marketing strategy for any publisher is the long-term editorial plan for the list. If much of the current output is either parochial to the UK or otherwise unsuitable for the export market, do you have a plan to produce any new lines or products that will be more attractive to international customers? For example, ELT publishers may have to consider producing editions of their books in American English in order to break into markets where US English predominates.

1.7.6 Language and culture

Export markets vary widely in the extent to which English language and culture are assimilated, and this can affect the way you prioritise markets. In Northern Europe and Scandinavia, for example, English is spoken and understood by large numbers of people, whereas in some Asian markets, such as Indonesia or Korea, only a few people in the street will be able to speak or read English. Ease of access to language may affect your decision on where to start your export effort.

1.7.7 Commitment

Commitment is a key issue. Your company can only succeed in export if the management commits to the market – strategically, editorially, and with strong and sustained support for the international sales and marketing effort.

1.7.8 Finance

As long as costs are understood well in advance, and budgeted for, the export plan should be easy to implement. Targets, timescales, and ways of measuring results need to be in place. Discounts, credit periods, pricing and stock control need to be carefully and continuously monitored – preferably in discussion with whoever is selling the books on the ground.

1.7.9 Pricing, discounts and mark-ups

The economic environment in export markets varies widely, from very low income countries in Asia and Africa to more prosperous European countries that enjoy very high standards and costs of living. It will be worthwhile familiarising yourself with the prevailing circumstances in any market you want to sell to. Discounts in markets such as the Philippines or Pakistan are traditionally very high, whereas Japanese and Northern European booksellers usually apply a healthy mark-up on the UK RRP to cover their costs, and consequently discounts are generally lower, though the trend in recent years has been for competitive pricing across the Euro zone which in turn has led to demands for higher discounts.

2   Export sales management

2.1   Models for export sales management

There are various models and degrees of engagement which publishers use to approach export markets, depending on the type of product being sold and the size of the potential market.

2.1.1   Passive/casual

Publishers who do not actively seek export business, but respond as necessary to enquiries and orders. This approach may be appropriate to poor and high-credit-risk markets for small and medium-sized publishers who want to concentrate their resources on better prospects. The poorer African and Asian countries fall into this category. Usually orders are supplied on pro-forma invoices (i.e., paid for in advance). Indirect export channels, such as UK-based exporters, wholesalers and library suppliers can also be helpful when using this model.

The passive approach can also be a cost-efficient way of testing promising markets, such as those in Eastern Europe. It involves little more than providing a back office resource for mailing and responding to queries. The use of the internet for electronic delivery of promotion material, and email generally, has made it a lot easier to adopt the passive/casual approach. However, it is ultimately limited in the amount of business it can generate.

2.1.2   Active open market

In this model, also known as selling direct, the publisher has no formal agency or distribution arrangements in the market, but sells to whichever retailers and wholesalers are available. The publisher manages the markets direct via telephone, fax, email, visits, and meetings at book fairs. This can be an effective method in smaller markets where the publisher has strong product lines that are in regular demand, and there are easily identifiable customers who respond to direct approaches. Despite the cost of travel, this can be the most profitable model for both publisher and retailer because there is no middleman in the supply chain. However, it does require a good deal of management and administrative time to keep it going. It can also be hard to achieve real volume without sustained local representation on the ground. This approach can also expose you to credit risk, without the prospect of any local help on the ground if things go wrong.

2.1.3   Agent/representative

Publishers' agents and representatives are commission-based freelance sales people who cover the markets of any given region. They are mainly sole traders and partnerships, who are either located locally or who make regular visits to the markets on behalf of a group of publishers. Most agents in this category are focused on trade-calling, while some do college-calling and library visits (although they will not do the latter unless they can identify sales via a local supplier). Representation can also be agreed with a larger publisher that has a sales team in place making regular visits to a market or region.

2.1.4   Agent/distributor

Full service, locally-based agency and distribution facilities are offered in some markets by either large, multinational groups, or independents such as UPS in Japan, APD in Singapore, or Research Press in India. This is a very effective method of entering the market, as your product is immediately positioned strongly alongside established lines via a well-established sales and distribution channel. However, to get the attention of these groups you need to be able to offer some sort of volume sales or exceptionally good niche product that fits their market positioning.

2.1.5 Salaried employee

Most common for larger publishers, but not unheard of for smaller companies, is to hire a local representative in major markets such as China and Japan, where local knowledge and presence is at a premium. A good base level of sales is required to make this economically viable.

2.1.6 Joint venture agency

This would involve a publisher making a turnkey deal with another, usually larger, group to represent them throughout the world. Bloomsbury, Faber and Little, Brown had such an arrangement with Penguin for a number of years. This strategy can resemble a co-publication deal, and has advantages for small lists that want to have a single point of entry into their international market. This sort of international presence involves mature marketing or distributor relationships, and a dedicated export team travelling regularly to the markets.

2.1.7 Multinational operation

Congratulations – you have built a global business! You have publishing, marketing, production and stockholding world-wide, according to market priorities. You will also have local-language operation and local profit-centre reporting to head office. But your CEO and CFO may still benefit from reading this Guide.

2.2 Committing to export: building and managing a network

Most successful exporting publishers operate a network made up of a mix of the above mechanisms, especially the first four. Whichever method or level of interaction with the market you decide on, the keys to success are found in *maintaining focus* on export priorities, *allocating resources to* develop sales (especially back office 'sales service' support), and building the *best possible relationships* with the key players for your list in the market. Managing agencies is a much more important part of the export job than appointing them. Whatever arrangement you have, make sure that you take the time to visit the agents and distributors regularly. As the Americans say, *'It pays to show up.'*

3 Selecting and managing agents and distributors

3.1 Kinds of agency

Most agency operations are defined by territory, and/ or product categories. The broadest divide is between trade and academic product. ELT and STM often dispense with agencies altogether because of their special needs or characteristics. Different market areas also commonly rely on different approaches: it is far more likely that you will be dealing direct with retailers and wholesalers in Northern Europe than East Asia, where local or travelling representation is more important.

3.1.1 UK-based agency

UK-based agents travel to the territory regularly, usually two or three times a year for the major markets, and report back to publishers regularly. Obviously UK-based agents are slightly easier to keep in touch with than those who are based overseas, but this can in turn lead them to be distanced from the markets they serve.

3.1.2 Locally or regionally-based agency

A locally or regionally based agency is advantageous for high-maintenance markets, where a constant local presence is needed (say for schools adoption business), or where credit is an issue. In the Indian sub-continent, for example, most publishers are represented by a local representative because the accounts often need high levels of service, and in particular credit chasing. Local representatives are also common in low-income markets, as they tend to be more cost-efficient than those based in the UK. Wherever they are located, export sales agencies may be either sole traders or partnerships. Others, such as Andrew Durnell Associates in Europe or Gunnar Lie & Associates in worldwide markets, are mature operations with large travelling sales forces.

3.1.3   Agent/distributor

Agent/distributors are based in or near the markets they serve, and are a popular solution to markets such as South East Asia, where customers require local stock and a local returns facility. Some agent/distributors operate on an exclusive basis, whereby all stock and orders go through them, others both hold stock and sell to third parties on commission. Non-exclusive distributors get preferential terms on discount and credit periods, but allow you to keep dealing with some accounts direct (with or without commission). Line distribution – taking on specific product lines – is also common in some markets, including Japan, where large retailers will take an exclusive on major titles such as dictionaries and encyclopaedias.

3.1.4   Agent vs. distributor

Deciding on whether to go the agent or distribution route depends on the following criteria:

- *Agents' pros and cons:* The agency model allows you control over prices and terms of sale. The best agents know their markets inside out, and enjoy good relationships with the key accounts. Their existing product lines lend credibility to your own books, and a short cut to established relationships. They can achieve quick results with low maintenance costs. However, commission agents have no real responsibility for your sales, and some will carry too many imprints to allow time to focus on your list. Agents are driven by commission, and tend to take a short-term view, offering limited scope for market development. Commission costs can become high as sales progress, but of course this is a sign of success.

- *Distributors' pros and cons:* Distributors are the best option if your customers have a need for ready stock – for example, if you publish fast-moving texts, trade, or schoolbooks. They are also useful for serving markets where you have a number of small customers that you do not want to service, for whatever reason (usually credit). The pressure of stockholding can drive sales and local promotion initiatives. There is more potential to grow organically, and to build market knowledge and local marketing/publishing initiatives. On the downside there may be some loss of control over pricing, and the cost of failure can be high: sorting out dead stock and bad debts with a distributor can prove much more expensive than terminating a commission agent. The distribution route can also leave you more vulnerable to exchange rate fluctuations.

- *Market politics:* The English-language book trade in export markets can be highly competitive, and this can create a political minefield for publishers, with various importers competing for your attention. Managing markets, especially open market models, can be tricky, and choosing the wrong distributor or agent is costly. However slick the pitch, always check with local customers to ensure that you are not hiring someone with a bad reputation. Your customers will not support you if you appoint someone they regard as unreliable. The success or failure of your sales depends on the quality of your agent's or distributor's relationships within the market. Problems with distributors include their trying to operate as retailers, giving poor service, offering ungenerous terms, or applying unreasonable mark-ups. Bad distributors can force retail customers to buy round via third parties, choose US editions of your titles, or simply not buy enough of your stock.

3.2   Appointing agents: criteria for selection

The following are some of the questions and issues you should consider raising when choosing potential agents:

- *Capacity:* Do they already represent too many publishers in your area? What is the size of their existing business: will your list be swallowed up in a morass of competing product? Or will they be overwhelmed by the demands of your list? Find out how many new titles they have to sell each year.

- *Capability:* Do they have enough staff and resources to cover their market effectively? Or are they a just a one man/woman band trying to cover too much?

- *Security:* Are they financially secure? If the agency is a partnership, check that the partners get on.

- *Cost:* Are their commission rates 10 per cent or more? Some agents insist on 12.5 per cent, but there is usually some flexibility in negotiations.

- *Category:* What are their category specialisations? Are their existing product lines complementary to your own? Or too similar? Publishers tend to look for agents in their field, but this can be counter-productive if the agent already represents all your competitors. It may pay not to follow the herd, and to take a chance on an emerging agent, or an established one trying to get into a new category.

- *Textbook and library calling:* If you have textbooks or library reference product, you will need someone to visit schools and colleges to win adoptions and sell to librarians. Few freelance representatives sell to libraries, because they are unlikely to see the commission on library supplier orders, but some will drop off sales material.

- *Call cycles:* How often do they call on their customers? Do they have a local presence, and/or language capability?

- *Interest level:* Have they checked the product? Are they keen and focused, or do they have a tepid, catch-all approach? Have they data on the market and their activities that they can give you?

- *Chemistry:* Put simply, do you like the people? Will working with them be fun? After all, few of us go into this business just for the money.

- *References:* They should be able to give you good references from their current roster of publishers and – more importantly – customers.

- *Reporting and communications:* Do they attend the Frankfurt and London book fairs? Do they attend other local book fairs? Will they attend your sales conferences/meetings? How often do they provide market reports?

3.3   Appointing a distributor: criteria for selection

Most of the criteria for appointing a distributor are the same as for agents (Section 3.2), with added emphasis on the following:

- *Security:* Is the company financially sound? Do they have good credit control, and enough working capital to fund their stockholding?

- *Technology:* Are they equipped to handle new technology, such as EDI and web-based selling? Have they invested in appropriate systems to manage and market your list effectively?

- *Stock control:* How do they manage their inventory? What is their policy on returns?

- *Mailing capacity:* Do they mail regularly in their territory, and are you expected to make a contribution?

- *Sales and marketing:* What sort of people and mechanisms do they have in place to give your list a presence in the market?

- *Pricing policy:* <u>Check the distributor's mark-up and pricing policy.</u> It is usual for overseas distributors and retailers to apply some sort of mark-up to cover shipping and warehousing costs. You should ensure that this is in line with the prevailing market norms.

3.4 Hiring agents and distributors: contractual issues

Well-drafted contracts are highly desirable with agents and distributors – especially for when things go wrong. Contracts with agents do not need to be very elaborate and, apart from those deals involving very substantial stock and credit risks, should not generally need to involve professional legal advisors. In many cases a simple memorandum of agreement is enough: after all, if the arrangement is not working it will soon become clear, and it is rarely worthwhile for either party to pursue expensive transnational legal action. However, contracts are useful for establishing a sound basis for working together and avoiding ambiguity. Any contract appointing an agent or distributor should clearly and accurately define the following:

- The parties making the agreement.

- The products covered (with some provision for future acquisitions and the digital dimension (see Section 3.10).

- The territories covered (with care – remember smaller territories like Brunei in South-East Asia, or Nepal/Sri Lanka in the Indian Subcontinent).

- The nature of exclusivity (does it include direct orders from individuals, or UK exporters?)

- Duration (2–3 years is the norm).

- The rights and duties of each party (for example, provision of promotion material, conference and book fair attendance).

The contract should also include provisions on the following:

- **Prices and discounts**, terms, fees, and agreements on any consignment deals if appropriate. For commission agents it is usual to agree a baseline of discounts and credit terms by territory. Any additional concessions can be agreed mutually.

- **Commission rates** for agents, and commission payment terms, usually quarterly in arrears and based on net invoiced sales. The commission section of the contract should also make provision for reduced or no commission on sales to designated 'house accounts', and for reduced commission on any special deals.

- **Notice period** for termination – usually six months for either party.

- **Applicable law:** usually this will be UK law.

- **Sales targets,** if applicable.

- **Costs of promotion:** Arrangements for handling costs for exhibitions, mailings and conference attendance.

- **Bad debts:** Most contracts make provision for the publishers to recover commission on bad debts after a specified period.

- **Returns:** Guidelines for allowable return ratios against turnover, and an understanding of how agents are allowed to authorise returns for third-party customers.

- **Exclusion of competitors:** Some publishers ask agents either to refrain from taking on specified competitors, or at least to refer any such plans to them for approval.

Above all, your agents' and distributors' contracts should include an element of flexibility, to allow for entrepreneurial initiatives – for example, on conference attendance or mailing costs, which can usually be mutually agreed on an *ad hoc* basis.

3.4.1 Hiring European agents

If you are hiring agents or distributors in Europe, you should make sure you are aware of the EU legislation affecting compensation due to agents. The Commercial Agents (Council Directive) Regulations 1993 is European law passed by Parliament that sets out the rights and obligations between commercial agents and their principals, and deals with remuneration due at termination of the agency contract. The Regulations contain provisions relating to the indemnity or compensation payable to a commercial agent on termination of his agency contract, and also to the validity of restraint of trade clauses. These regulations are likely to affect every publisher appointing sales agents in Europe. For more information visit website of the National Archives of the UK Government's legislation: www.legislation.gov.uk/uksi/1998/2868/contents/made.

3.5 Setting up a new agency/distributor

On appointing a new agent or distributor, you should do the following to help establish the agreement on a sound basis:

- Make an announcement of the appointment in the trade press in the UK, and locally if appropriate.

- Write to key customers in the territory informing them of the appointment.

- Arrange training/product briefing for the agent's staff.

- Send sales data, including all historical and current sales by account and by title.

- Ensure that your agent knows their service contacts, both in-house and in your distribution centre.

- List the agents and their territories in your catalogues and on your website and keep them regularly updated.

3.6   Keys to successful agency management

Many publishers find that appointing agents and distributors is much easier than managing them. Here are some guidelines for management:

- *Regular contact:* Agents should be given one contact person for service and product queries. Telephone calls to agents should be made regularly to review sales, discuss promotions, or just shoot the breeze. Email is, of course, an excellent way of staying in touch too.

- *Support and service:* Especially in Management Information Systems (MIS). Agents need monthly sales printouts; prompt payment of commission; regular supplies of promotional information, and good liaison and support on credit issues.

- *Incentives:* Agree targets and cash incentives direct to staff/representatives if possible.

- *Planning and reporting systems:* Try to agree on reports, budgets and trip plans before the start of your financial year. Encourage your agents to report back regularly on the market, and monitor their performance yourself.

- *Promotional support:* Suggest promotions, and respond positively to any promotion initiatives from the agent.

- *Be flexible:* Agree special prices on books with local appeal, and consider 'marketorial' publishing initiatives that address specific market opportunities in the agent's territories.

- *Be the best they deal with:* Ask which publishers gives them the best support and service, and try to emulate or better them.

3.7　Motivating agents

Here are some additional suggestions for getting the most out of your export agents:

- *Arrange training visits for agents and staff* to your head office and warehouse – based on achievement of incentive targets if possible. People enjoy visiting the UK, and it gives you the chance to introduce your agent to your staff.

- *Invite your agents to an international sales conference.* Publishers' UK sales conferences are often unsuitable for export agents and distributors because there is such a strong focus on the home market, and too much detail on individual titles. Arranging an international day or half-day, either in addition to or as an adjunct to your domestic conference, is a good way to get your export people together with your editorial and marketing teams to focus on international sales. The meeting will also give you the opportunity to do some PR and show appreciation to your export team, with dinners and outings sporting and/or cultural events, or shopping trips. It is also a good idea to encourage participation by inviting attendees to give presentations of their markets. Consider making presentations of prizes and awards to your agents at the conference too.

- *Treat your export agents with respect,* no matter how small their contribution to your sales, and thank them for their efforts. Treat them as far as possible as extension of your in-house sales and marketing team. Ask their advice, encourage them to take initiatives, and involve them in product development or promotional planning as much as you can.

3.8   Monitoring agent performance

Monitoring agent performance is relatively simple if you have good MIS reporting systems of sales figures by territory. These should be checked monthly, and any anomalous shortfalls or spikes in turnover should be flagged up and discussed with the agent over the telephone or by email. Visiting the market and getting feedback from customers is also useful as a way of supporting and monitoring your agents.

3.9   Troubleshooting agents and distributors

The following are some common problems that you might encounter with your agents:

- *Agent takes on your major competitor:* You can include an exclusion clause in your agreement, whereby the agent refers to you before taking on any potential new clients who might conflict with your list. In some cases, it may make sense to agree to an agent taking on a competing list, as it may build their critical mass in your category, allowing them to focus more closely on your market segment.

- *Agent fails to sell:* This may be as a result of number of factors, not all of which are necessarily the fault of the agent. It may be that your product offer is not appropriate for the market, or your catalogue mailings have not landed. It is best to find out exactly what is going on before you complain.

- *Agent dies, becomes ill, or gets taken over:* Depending on whether your contract is assignable or not, you may want to terminate at this point.

- *Your business gets bought out:* Congratulations, but be aware that you will usually be required to compensate any agencies terminated as a result of the sale for any loss of earnings. This is a legal requirement in EU countries (see Section 3.4.1).

- *Market collapses:* This worst-case scenario is usually a result of regional or national financial crashes, such as occurred in Asia in 1997, or of natural or man-made disasters such as the Asian tsunami in 2004. The best response here is to negotiate extended credit and retrospective discount credits with key customers, and wait for the situation to improve again.

- *Customer complaints about agents,* and failure to communicate are all problems that should be resolved in the first instance by discussion, and as a last resort by termination (see Section 3.11).

Relationships with distributors can become strained by credit issues, overstocks, or returns requests. Stock is the most likely cause of problems, and for this reason publishers should be wary of big opening stock orders, especially if these are on consignment. In all cases, negotiation is the best way to resolve problems. Continuity and stability in export marketing arrangements are worth working towards because of the long-term nature of market development. Terminating agreements is costly in both time and resources. It can also create ill will in the market, and loss of reputation, as well as credit and stock problems. Stock transfers in particular can be costly, and there is a risk of the distributor dumping your stock in the market at low prices. Legal action should be regarded as an absolute last resort as the sums involved are unlikely to justify the cost and inconvenience of pursuing a legal case abroad.

3.10   Digital sales in the international arena

It is worth mentioning at this stage that some agent/distributors are vigorously pursuing either the rights to sell digital/e-books alongside physical books, or a percentage commission on sales of digital versions of publishers' product in the contracted territories.

- The argument from the distributors' side is that sales of digital/e-books, in a territory where they have been granted exclusivity on the sales of physical books, benefit from the promotional activities of those same physical books, and that some form of compensation is due to the distributor for the efforts put into the 'product' in whatever form the consumer then decides to buy it.

- The counter argument is that digital/e-books are sold and promoted in very different channels and that it is notoriously difficult to accurately say where the sales effort has come from.

A degree of compromise is likely to have to be worked out between publishers and agents/distributors working in 'exclusive' territories where digital/e-book sales begin to make an impact on the overall sales, if only in order to protect the good will that exists in promoting the publishers' existing lists of physical books.

3.11   Terminating agents' contracts

Contracts with agents come to an end for various reasons, most commonly because publishers are dissatisfied with the performance of the agent, or ironically, because the agent has done so well that the publisher feels that they can go it alone. Some agents have been known to terminate publishers, either because they cannot make the list work for them, or because the publisher does not support them adequately. Usually contracts are terminated by negotiation, and provisions on notice periods or compensation are mutually agreed. Most contracts stipulate that notice of termination should be given in writing, preferably by registered post.

4 Exporting digital products

4.1 Introduction

The launch of the Sony Reader in the USA in late 2006 created shockwaves the industry is still dealing with. The reality is that even the most thoughtful of industry analysts stood little chance of predicting the momentous change this device heralded.

Since that US launch we have seen Sony push into the UK, we have had Amazon utilise their global reach to launch arguably the biggest service in the world and of course we have had Apple drop books alongside their world-beating music sale system iTunes®.

With the introduction of Apple we have added commercial complexities through the agency model and seen a reworking of traditional trading patterns... retailers are now publishing and publishers are now retailing. Somewhere in amongst all this bookshops are finding their place – the transatlantic marquee names of Borders, Barnes & Noble, Waterstones, and WH Smith sell digital products on either a standalone or digital partnership basis.

Google are now both selling direct and also powering sales for indies in the USA and with their global reach add a compelling third way to the established tech giants of Amazon and Apple.

And of course we now talk about companies in the digital sphere that very few knew about three or four years ago – if indeed they existed at that point. If Kobo (www.kobobooks.com) and Overdrive (www.overdrive.com)

are arguably the leaders in this category, it would be foolish to assume they will hold the floor to themselves forever.

In less than five short years the world of book publishing and retailing has been through what's starting to look like a revolution. And most of us realise this is only the start of it.

Living and trading in the UK, and being an industry strongly focussed on the UK and USA markets, we can often forget about the impact these movements have beyond those territories. But the reality is digital has ripple effects and is challenging some of publishing's longest held and most cherished traditions. This short introduction is an attempt to give you a simple guideline to some of these effects and plot a straight line through the trade's new realities.

4.2   Physical trade and territorial rights

When a book is released into the global market by a UK publisher it usually has physical rights attached to it in one of the following ways:

- *World English/all language rights:* the publisher has obtained global rights to sell that book anywhere in the world.

- *UK/Commonwealth and US split rights:* the publisher acquired world rights in a book, has retained rights in their territory of creation (the UK) but sold US territorial rights to a US publisher. In this case the open market territories are usually shared between the two publishers.

- *UK/Commonwealth and US/other territory split rights:* meaning as well as selling rights to a US company, the UK publisher has also sold rights to another publisher to publish in a specific territory (for example, if the book has a strong Australian theme they may sell rights to an Australian publisher to publish a local edition in Australia).

- *UK/Commonwealth only:* the publisher has acquired exclusive rights to sell the work in the UK and Commonwealth territories, and the non-exclusive right to sell the work in the open market. Europe may or may not be exclusive, depending on what the publisher has negotiated with the author. A US publisher will have acquired exclusive US rights and non-exclusive open market rights direct from the author.

These four basic patterns of rights are then communicated out to the global book market, most often via electronic feeds through data aggregators (or wholesalers). These data aggregators (such as Nielsen or Bowker) then communicate them in turn out to individual retailers.

Most UK publishers will then sell their books internationally in one of three ways:

OUP

- *Sell to a Group (or sister) company* located in an export territory (for example Penguin UK would sell physical copies of their books to Penguin Australia to sell in the local market).

- *Offer their titles to a local distributor* who will assume local distribution rights on a representational basis.

- *Sell directly into an export market* (for example into the open market territories of Europe) to individual retailers or wholesalers.

With each of these three options for sales publishers will hold multiple relationships and in turn manage large numbers of accounts and attendant administration. If you want to visualise it think of a traditional family tree… the publisher sits at the top and through an increasingly complex web of relationships ends up maintaining both immediate and more distant relationships with a huge number of partners. By the time you reach the bottom of this imagined publishing family tree, the publisher may well be dealing with hundreds of relationships across multiple territories.

It is important to note at this stage that restrictions on trading titles into certain territories have been easy to uphold for much of the history of publishing and territorial rights. This is because the cost of sending physical copies of books around the world helps to reinforce the agreements made between publishers – there has historically been little attraction for say an Australian bookshop to source a US edition of a title if the UK publisher releases an edition locally due to the costs of shipping. In other words, physical distance has been a major factor in upholding territorial agreements.

4.3   Digital trade and territorial rights

When dealing in digital sales there is one obvious but often misunderstood fact. Physical trade involves sending real copies (at real expense) across geographical boundaries. Digital trade eliminates geographical boundaries and to a very large extent eliminates the cost of shipping (leaving in its place the cost of file hosting/transmission).

There are several interlinked and incredibly important points that flow from this:

- Physical distance between publishers and their retailers is no longer a factor (a publisher is no longer shipping physical copies across geographical spaces, file copies are now transmitted electronically at extremely low cost). The side-effect of this is shipping costs (traditional reinforcers of territorial rights) are taken out of the equation.

- Electronic/digital territorial information is now crucial in determining sales territories (without the extra barrier to trade of geographical space, retailers will now be solely driven by the electronic feeds on territorial data).

- Electronic/digital territorial information still has certain drawbacks, namely in the way the information cannot "flex" and is locked into its attendant ISBN.

- With the elimination of physical copies and geographical space from the sales chain, bandwidth (in terms of storage space or a physical capacity) ceases to become an issue.

In plain English the publisher family tree we discussed above suddenly looks very different, with publishers now either reaching their end retailers (at the localised store or book chain level) through small numbers of digital wholesalers, or reaching their end consumer (i.e., the person who actually buys their digital files) through massive globally reaching digital accounts (such as Amazon). The immediate effect is fewer direct relationships to reach consumers.

Digital creates a situation where retailers with a global reach have the ability to easily trade globally (without cost barriers), and will want to do that wherever possible. Fewer wholesalers and fewer direct retail partners will potentially effect the sales that multiple suppliers were needed to deliver in the past.

4.4   The supply chain

The supply chain to deliver this looks markedly different to the physical example.

- *The publisher is likely to have far fewer direct relationships*. This is because:

    - physical storage and capacity is no longer an issue. Once a partner has the financial backing and technical ability to create file storage and hosting services they are able to trade those globally.
    - the costs and technical knowledge create barriers to entry. This means fewer digital wholesalers will deliver the same reach as far more physical wholesalers would be required to deliver.

- *Cost barriers to entry for retailers* mean only the very dedicated or cash rich can think about creating a retailer-owned solution.

So you should expect to work with a limited number of wholesalers who are able to effectively deliver your content to the end consumer, and similarly, expect to see a limited number of direct retailer relationships for your content.

International wholesalers and retailers will use the publisher's territorial information to determine where they can sell – it is now incredibly important for the publisher to always have the correct information attached to their ISBNs. Without it they will either lose sales or end up infringing on another publisher's rights.

The information on territories is contained in a set of data collectively described as "metadata". In one sense this is nothing more than a digital expression for what we used to call bibliographic data. In another, it is however the crowningly important way for a publisher to succeed or fail digitally.

4.5   Metadata

Metadata is the information that accompanies a digital file (the actual text of a book) in its travels through cyberspace. It's the publicly facing information that finds its way onto digital catalogues (i.e., what you see when you look at a digital file on Amazon or the iBooks store) - pieces of data such as title, price, synopsis, publication date, author etc.

However, behind the scenes, it's also the information the retailer (or wholesaler) uses in determining (amongst other things) which territories a file may be sold in. It is absolutely key that your metadata accurately reflects the territories in which you have the rights to sell. Going back to the start of this guide, if you have sold off US rights for your title and retained UK and Commonwealth then the ISBN you use for that title MUST tell your retail partners they may not sell in the USA (the US publisher will in turn create an ISBN with metadata attached that will be available for sale only within the USA).

OUP - single ISBN's as through sister companies.

Chanty - limited?

If any part of your territorial metadata is wrong then you will end up losing sales or infringing on your partnering publishers' rights. It is not possible for your retailers to interpret your metadata in any other way than that in which you transmit it to them. The systems for digital sales that each retailer uses are incredibly black and white – and so it's incredibly important for you to get your metadata right.

The good news is that for most publishers, their digital metadata will faithfully mirror the territorial information for their physical edition. So long as the basic information surrounding your physical edition has been recorded and stored correctly it should be relatively easy to map that across to any digital edition.

However, it is incredibly important for a publisher to dig back into their records to ensure they are correctly reporting their rights. Errors that may be unnoticed in the physical supply chain will be glaring in digital and so you can not emphasise enough the importance of going back to your source records to check your information.

4.6   Commercial models

Earlier in this section we mentioned the lack of "flex" inherent in metadata, particularly as it relates to territorial rights. It is not possible for a publisher to attach multiple sales rights to a title in a territory. Plainly speaking when a publisher releases metadata for a title, it is not possible for them to allow multiple entities to claim sales rights in any one territory – the old models of Group or international export trade (where a sister company, an exclusive distributor, or indeed multiple retailers could buy your product and resell it in the territory and claim the sale proceeds) are almost impossible to replicate through digital retailer systems and digital metadata.

This is because a retailer can only assign one publisher (and hence, seller of record) for each digital ISBN in their system. So in practise the publisher can (and through the current metadata and system limitations, must) assume primary rights for the sale of their title in any territory for which they have the right.

Whilst this allows the publisher in theory to now sell direct into any global territory for which they have the right it is not necessarily that simple. The publisher now needs to consider whether they have enough local market knowledge to effectively promote and market that title directly in the territory.

The example would be a small UK publisher who traditionally sold into say the USA or Australia either through an exclusive distributor or direct to local stores. Through the combined effects of the global reach of digital wholesalers and retailers, and the current limitations of metadata feeds, this publisher can now sell their titles direct into the USA or Australia – bypassing their distributor and retailer partners to effect the sale and collect the proceeds themselves.

The question is whether they have the knowledge to effectively market the digital edition in those territories – you could mount a strong argument that local distributors and retailers are vital for this purpose. Equally you could argue the opposite – that this is the time for publishers with global reach to rethink localised marketing strategies according to the new digital realities.

There is no right answer to this question and different publishers do it differently – some simply claim the sale and rely on global marketing to promote their titles locally, some offer an income share to local partners to continue presence for their physical editions and to guarantee local promotional work. Whichever way the publisher goes this is something they must consider carefully.

The other element of the commercial model the publisher needs to consider is agency and reseller. Agency has been a sales model pursued by various publishers in the USA and UK since 2010. Some retailers/ agents will not offer you the choice between models, and will insist on one or the other. It is also the case that your title may be sold on differing models dependent on which territory it is being sold in.

If you wish to sell under differing models and in differing territories the important point here is to ensure that your metadata is able to handle this complexity. If you choose to work under agency it is often expedient to have local currency pricing – it follows then that you may need to set various agency prices, as well as either a global or even localised reseller price. It's vital you have the ability to do this through your metadata, and equally vital your agents/retailers are able to correctly allocate prices to territories.

And of course the knock on issue is ensuring your own systems are able to effectively handle the resulting multi-currency reporting you may be receiving. _ *divisions*

This is a complex area and one that you need to put some thought into. The ramifications of faulty metadata when it comes to pricing and territorial commercial models are significant, and so this is probably the one area you want to think about most carefully before progressing.

4.7 Summary

In summary, the key points for any publisher looking to sell their products globally are these:

- *Clean metadata.* It is the lifeblood of any digital transaction and vital in export sales. Without it you really have nowhere to go in this environment.

- *Fewer, more specialised partners*. You can reach the same breadth of audience with fewer partners than are required in physical. So choose them carefully and make sure you do so with a global outlook.

- *Direct selling*. Under a globalised approach to digital sales the originating publisher can sell directly into any territory they have rights for (without the need of traditional export partners). This opens a host of issues and is not a cut and dried question – the publisher must carefully consider their traditional partnerships and the value they bring around local knowledge to the publishing value chain before deciding which way to go.

5 Export sales promotion 1: personal selling

5.1 Sales Trip

There are three main categories of sales trip:

- Visiting your agents and customers individually.
- Book fair attendance.
- PA trade delegation.

In all cases the principles of a successful sales trip are more or less the same.

DO ...

- ***Be prepared:*** Prepare yourself well in advance for your trip. Arrange appointments at least four weeks before you are due to travel. Find out which, if any, of your books are selling in the market and to whom. Try to learn at least a couple of words of the local language – at least 'hello', 'please', 'thank you' and 'excuse me', and maybe the numbers from one to ten. Read something about the history and current political, economic and social climate of the countries you are visiting. Buy some maps, and try to get an idea of where the cities and districts you are visiting are located in relation to each other, so that you do not find yourself criss-crossing town in taxis.

- ***Time management:*** Make a travel plan that works for both those you are visiting and you. Research the best times to visit the market, and check that you are not visiting in the middle of key selling season for your customers. They will not want to to spend much time with you if they are at their busiest time of year. Choose a time to suit them, not you. Try to avoid extremes of weather conditions, and any public holidays. Plan your time carefully to avoid having to rush around six appointments in one day, or being caught out with too much costly time on your hands. Remember to leave plenty of time for airport to city transfers and hotel check-ins.

- *Keep costs down:* Books are low-margin items, so it is best to avoid travelling in the style of a senior corporate potentate. To keep costs down, travel Economy, use the airport buses or trains, and get your agent or a friendly bookseller to recommend a reasonably priced hotel – they can sometimes get you special rates.

- *Be generous:* Try to invite agents, distributors and major customers to lunch or dinner, and take small gifts. These can range from tea or chocolate, to ties and bottles of Scotch, depending on your budget, and the country you are visiting. Remember that, apart from alcohol, it is usually cheaper to buy your gifts before you get to the airport.

DO NOT...

- *Expect instant results:* Concentrate on building relationships and your understanding of the markets rather than asking for orders.

- *Let customers pick you up from the airport* unless you have known them for a long time. Allowing new customers to do this can create an obligation that you may not want to fulfil down the line.

- *Turn up in markets unannounced or at short notice,* you will just irritate your customers and waste everyone's time.

- *Try not to pack too much into one trip.* It is possible to visit eight cities in two weeks, but you are unlikely to be in good enough shape to work effectively by the end of the first week. Shorter trips are usually more productive. Clock-watching during a meeting can create a bad impression. Leaving yourself extra time allows you to let meetings run on into lunch or dinner invitations – usually a good sign. Use any unexpected free time to browse local bookshops, checking prices and getting an idea of the pattern of demand on the ground.

5.2   Bookseller agendas

You have made it from the airport to town, checked into your hotel, and found your way to your customer. What next? Here are some suggestions as to how to approach meetings with importers:

- *Pre-trip planning:* You should have with you any necessary information to support your meeting. It is a good idea to have a customer data sheet (one for each of those attending) for your meeting with all the basic information such as discount, credit status, turnover both in the year to date and over the last couple of years, top title sales, dues, and if your customer is looking after the market for you then all of this should be available by account and/or market. By all means have this on your laptop, but do not rely on that alone.

- *Controlling the meeting:* You should have a clear idea of what you want out of the meeting. The usual opening comment is 'How's business?'. Describe the purpose of your visit, which could be to present new product, get feedback, build your knowledge of the needs of end-user customers, offer promotional support and ideas, or to resolve any problems.

- *Discuss sales year to date and year on year:* Why are they up, down, or flat? What is their sell-through and stock position like on your product?

- *Account queries:* Sort any credit issues and claims early on in the meeting, but avoid getting bogged down in detail with small invoice anomalies.

- *Discuss market conditions:* Ask about price points, mark-ups, library budgets, and any other relevant trends.

- *Make the sales presentation:* Open and close on your strongest books, and weight your presentation to customers' requirements. Try to sell promotion packages with books, and avoid overselling key books to too many customers. Discuss any exclusives if appropriate.

- *Review order:* Check order reference, shipping instructions, backorder/dues requirements. Confirm discounts and terms. Check for any backlist requirements.

- *Discuss the competition:* Ask who is doing what well or badly. Who are the best suppliers they deal with, and why? Can you emulate them?

- *Promotion issues:* Update catalogue mailing record; cover book fairs, exhibitions, and point-of-sale (POS) displays and consumer ads. If appropriate, discuss publicity drives, reading groups, and author tours.

- *Service issues:* Samples, spreads, e-delivery. Can you supply catalogues via their shipper? Are there any joint promotions you can do together?

- *Sales targets:* Suggest incentives with retrospective discounts, or free books, and visits to the UK for training, or visits as rewards for reaching sales targets.

- *Close:* Thank, and review meeting and check notes.

- *Follow up* on all points on your return, by email, and as soon as possible, preferably within a week or two.

A quick way to remember all of this is to think of your **MISSION** in each meeting, particularly important if you or your customer are time-pressed:

Market Intelligence – use the meeting to gain knowledge of what is happening in the market in general and your customer specifically

Issues – tackle and resolve any problems that either you or your customer have

Sales history – go through figures and analyse and understand what they mean

Sales targets – make clear what you would like from your customer in the next period or year

Information on product – clear succinct presentation of relevant titles, series or ranges

Offers – special discounts, incentives, promotions

Notes – make clear notes of what has been agreed or offered, so that these can be followed up and can be a permanent record if anybody else needs to take action later

5.3   Persuasive personal selling vs. order-taking

If your product is a red-hot certainty – say a Booker prize-winning novel, or an essential academic reference book – you will get orders regardless of the quality of your personal selling effort. With other books, you could just turn up, show your products and hope for the best: you might even get some business. But good selling technique will get more orders: after all, there are over 200,000 titles published in the UK and the US every year, by thousands of publishers. International customers have a huge choice of options when it comes to what to stock. What persuades them to buy your books? Obviously product quality is a big factor, but in areas where this is more or less equal, other factors such as discounts, credit periods, promotional support, and flexibility on returns allowances for dead stock are factors. Perhaps the biggest difference of all is made by the quality of the relationship that you build with your customers.

Bookselling is generally a low-margin, high-cost business. Most international customers are in the business for reasons other than to get rich. One of the compensations for them is to enjoy friendships with those they deal with. This can take time, but it's worth making the time to entertain your customers and talk about things other than business. Most experienced representatives and sales managers will agree that successful selling is 90 per cent about establishing good relationships with key customers. How can this be done? Here are some suggestions:

- *Be fair:* In negotiations and trading practice, do not try to squeeze your customer too hard, nor let them bully you into giving more discount than you need to. Hopefully your research will have forearmed you with the correct going rates for discounts. Be very clear about terms; stick to them, and be quick to resolve any service problems.

- *Share trade gossip:* Trade gossip; who's in and who's out in the market and the publishing scene in the UK is a source of fascination to most people in the international book trade. Many international customers like to keep up to date with developments in the UK. Ask what's going on in their market, and talk about your competitors.

- *Take it easy:* Relax, and chat about the weather, football, music, or whatever. Give your customers time – do not rush them or pressure them to make quick decisions. Letting your customers talk is a great way of both making friends with them and learning about the market.

- *Do not go for 'quick kill' sales:* It might work once, but you are unlikely to get repeat orders. Do not overstock your customers. In some markets, it is easy to sell more or less the same stock to several customers, who then try to sell it on to the same customers. Try to get a feel for the market potential for your key titles, and tell your customers if you think they are taking on too much stock.

- **Be creative about promotion ideas:** If you notice a promotional bind-up or spinner from one of your competitors, suggest that you do the same. Ask them how they promote your list, and try to think up ways of supporting them. This might mean new selling materials or a price promotion.

- **Be respectful:** It is surprising how quickly some English people can revert to colonial type when they go abroad. Old-fashioned, colonial style-selling, whether it be setting up a display of your books in a hotel suite and inviting customers to visit, or playing the great white chief is unlikely to work today. Try to find out about local etiquette, such as the correct way to present a business card with two hands in Asia, and make an effort to fit in with local customs on food, greetings and politeness.

5.4   Market feedback and market development

Giving and making use of market feedback is one of the most important parts of the export sales effort.

- Ask your agents for reports on how your product is received in their markets.

- Ask distributors and major retailers for their thoughts on your product, and how it can be made more appealing to their customers.

- Set up meetings for your editorial and marketing staff with key export people, especially if they are visiting from overseas, to discuss what works and what does not work in their markets.

You can then shape your product and promotional initiatives accordingly, and enjoy the benefits of the 'virtuous circle' a shown in Figure 5.4 overleaf.

Figure 5.4: The Export Sales Virtuous Circle:
How working closely with agents and customers drives growth

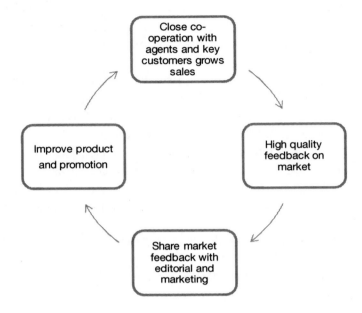

5.5 Creating special versions of books for export

Creating or modifying products for specific market opportunities – sometimes known as 'versioning' – is an excellent way of growing international sales, and in some cases it may be essential. Versioning takes various forms, depending on the product sector and market requirements.

5.5.1 International Student Editions

Publishers of academic, STM and ELT textbooks often create special low-priced editions, known as International Student Editions (ISEs), of their texts for sale to students in low-income countries – particularly Eastern Europe, Asia and Africa. Most ISEs are paperbacks produced to a lower specification than the original edition, with cheaper paper stock and plain one- or two-colour jackets suggesting value. Some publishers create ISEs by simply reducing the list price of their texts and running on additional copies for appropriate markets; changing the livery is not always essential.

The conditions required for a successful ISE programme include the following:

- An adoption for your textbook on a course with relatively large numbers of students.
- A low-income, or low-price market environment where the original edition would either not win the adoption or risks piracy, parallel importation of another edition, or photocopying.
- A strong partnership with a local college distributor or retailer(s) to sell the book in.
- A sound profit and loss analysis of the ISE's unit cost, net selling price, print run and projected sales.

5.5.2   Versioning trade books

Trade titles are produced in special editions by the larger publishers. These most commonly take the form of either Trade Paperbacks (C formats) for the larger Commonwealth markets of Australia, Canada and South Africa, or mass market paperbacks (A formats), commonly referred to as export or open market editions for early release into European and Asian markets to compete with US editions of the same title, or to combat piracy in markets such as India. Export editions' covers and prices are tailored to suit local requirements or sensibilities. To make any export editions work, close co-operation and advance planning with relevant key distributors are needed to ensure that everyone knows the quantities they will be required to take. Belly bands and stickers promoting the book in either local languages or local prices are favoured by some distributors and retailers, notably in Japan and Europe. These are usually produced by the reseller, and can be printed either locally or by the publishers.

5.5.3   Versioning illustrated books

Covers, measurements, and references are routinely changed for sales of co-editions to US publishers, and some of these practices may be required by customers in other markets. Your Australian distributor may be able to sell more at a lower price with a reduced specification cover, for example. It may also be possible to encourage distributors and non-book retailers to take quantities of your book by applying their logo to the cover.

5.6 Attending book fairs and exhibitions

The most important international book fairs for export customers are Frankfurt, London, BookExpo America (BEA), and Bologna, in that order. Frankfurt is a must-attend, as is increasingly London. BEA is worth doing if you want to get to know the USA, although you will find most distributors and publishers heavily focused on their domestic affairs. Bologna is a children's fair, with a major emphasis on rights sales and eating delicious food.

The major regional fairs are also worth considering: Beijing, Abu Dhabi, Cairo, Moscow, and Tehran all have their fans. It pays to check with someone who has attended in the past to see whether it is worth going. Some fairs, like Cape Town or the New Delhi World Book Fair, are determinedly local events, where your market contacts may be too distracted by dealing with their own customers to give you much of their time. For the contact details of all the major fairs see Appendix 8.

Most of the advice above for making sales visits to customers in their territories applies to attending book fairs. Here are some more tips for getting the most out of them:

- *Plan early:* Book your stand early, and make sure you understand the costs involved. Peripheral items such as stand fixtures and furniture are often charged at exorbitant prices. Make appointments with key customers and agents well in advance. Encourage your agents and distributors to bring their own key customers to your stand.

- *Have an agenda for each appointment:* Every meeting should have an objective, even if it is only a special stock order. Remember your MISSION: use the agenda items in Section 5.2 to map out a rough plan of each meeting.

- *Keep costs down:* Stay in modest hotels and share a stand to reduce costs. UKTI offers grants to SMEs to exhibit at some trade fairs; the PA provides a good turnkey exhibition service and the IPG also offers stand space for even the smallest publishers at London and Frankfurt.

- *Entertain:* Make time to take your key customers to lunch or dinner during the fair, or consider having a small drinks party on your stand. Remember that you are still 'on parade' at such events and that what you say and do will reflect on both you and your publisher.

- *Make time for smaller customers:* It's tempting to block out all your time for major customers, agents and distributors, but this may not always be the best strategy. After all, assuming you are working with them in the right way, there should be little to discuss apart from a review of sales figures and presentation of key new products. It often makes more sense to reserve time for smaller customers from peripheral markets, where sales may not justify a visit, but who come to the fair with the intention of buying. Giving time to such customers can prove more rewarding in terms of orders.

- *Promote your business:* Use the excitement of the occasion to get some sales momentum by offering special terms and promotions. Encourage customers to order at the fair. Consider having modest giveaways of pens or other gimmicks, more substantial (lightweight) gifts for important partners, or run a competition. Make the visit to your stand memorable in some way; for your customer it will be one of so many in a crowded schedule.

- *Keep calm:* The excitement and hubbub of the fair, especially Frankfurt, combined with the traditional late night carousing with colleagues and customers, can cause frayed nerves and inspire intemperate comments at meetings. Most export sales managers and directors can remember some nightmare meetings when they have said things they have later regretted. Frankfurt and London are not particularly good places to introduce major strategic changes, such as sackings of agents, for the same reason. It is always best to resist the temptation to start shouting, and agree to fix things in another, less feverish forum.

- *Network:* Of course, this is the essence of a book fair. Check out and introduce yourself to your larger competitors, and get hold of their catalogues. You can often learn something about a new agent or distributor from the back pages. Seminars and parties are another opportunity to get to know more people, so make sure you make the most of them.

For further information on international book fairs, refer to the *PA Guide to International Book Fairs*.

6 Export sales promotion II: mailing

6.1 Broad categories of mailing

Mailing to, and in co-operation with, your key accounts to support their sales of your list and joint promotions is a critical element of export strategy. There are four broad categories of mailing:

6.1.1 Mailing to agents, distributors and key customers

Bulk copies of your sales materials and samples of key titles should be mailed regularly to key customers and agents. A mailing database holding individual customers' requirements should be held in-house. In most cases you should mail what your customers request, but beware multiple copy requests from low-value markets. Some accounts will ask for 20 or 30 copies of your catalogues when they have little or no capacity to sell enough of your product to justify this cost. Clean and update your mailing list regularly to control costs. It is a good idea to offer your distributors and key customers 'overprints' of your sales material for special mailings and exhibitions, and send PDFs for adapting and local printing (hopefully at their cost).

6.1.2 Academic and end-user mailings

Academic and professional publishers need to get their material in front of their end customers, be they academics, professionals or librarians. Items mailed can include seasonal catalogues, single product leaflets and subject lists. Samples also fall into this category. Building end-user databases can be done in-house using directories such as *World of Learning*, but it is also common for publishers to use mailing houses.

6.1.3   Joint mailings

For joint mailings, costs are shared for mailing a subject promotion or bundled deal. They may involve local-language adaptations of your material, or overprints. Joint mailings have the benefit of better accuracy, because you are using a locally sourced mailing list as well as lower mailing costs.

6.1.4   Emailing and telemarketing

Email and web-based platforms represent an excellent low-cost resource for export promotion, but you should always ask your customers' permission to use email to send promotional material. You can also try to link your website with the sites of academic communities in your subject areas.

Telemarketing is used to sell high-ticket items such as major reference titles, journals and directories, but this can be a costly method. Sales presentations to the sales teams of your agents and larger customers can be a successful way of raising your profile if you arrange these. It is possible to research library collections on the web, and do your own telemarketing by calling librarians direct, but you should reserve this method for your most high-value items.

6.2   Mailing materials

The most important part of your mailing armoury is your seasonal new books announcement list and Advance Information Sheets (AIs). AIs are crucial for trade publishers, who should collect them along with jackets in sales kits for mailing, or better still, emailing to agents and key customers; timing is critical to ensure inclusion in key distributors' own catalogues or sales cycles. The AIs should contain the following:

- Publisher's logo.
- Name of author(s), editor, illustrator, as appropriate.
- Title and sub-title, and series title where relevant.

- Publication date.
- Suggested retail price.
- ISBN.
- Number of pages and illustrations.
- Format and binding(s).
- Language.
- Two or three key selling points.
- Brief summary of contents, indicating localities where relevant.
- Brief details of the author(s) or editor: including where they are from and where they live.
- Intended readership.
- Promotional details: serialisation, press, TV & radio features, launches, etc.
- Reviews and recommendations: brief quotations from respected, named sources.
- Cover, author photograph or other appropriate image.
- Publisher's contact details.
- Distributors' contact details.

Make sure that your seasonal and subject catalogues include the following, on either the front or back pages:

- Listings of international agents, distributors and (where appropriate) stockists and their territories.
- The names of contact people for export customers in both your office and distribution centre with international formatted telephone numbers (+44 (0)20 xxxx xxxx for London numbers for instance).
- Subject lines for academic titles: the more categories you can place a book in, the more likely it is to get sales.

Keep mailing costs low by reducing the extent and paper weight of your catalogues.

6.2.1 Export promotion materials

- *Creating special materials:* Your UK catalogues will usually work acceptably as an export selling tool; however, in some cases, bespoke catalogues for export will make sense. For example, some customers like to have complete stocklists as a reference. Use email, the internet and/or CDs to make these available.

- *Using the internet* for electronic delivery of your product information and order forms is an excellent method of supporting your customers. Ideally they should be able to use your site to incorporate your sales information into their own subject catalogues and promotional material.

6.3 Working with UK-based exporters

Whether you are a trade or academic publisher, working with and through third-party suppliers in the UK is an important part of the export job. These come in two types, the mainstream wholesalers and UK exporters/library suppliers.

6.3.1 The wholesalers

The two major players are Bertrams (www.bertrams.com) and Gardners (www.gardners.com). They have both enjoyed steady growth in their export business over the past few years. The main reason for this is the convenience of consolidating orders through one or two suppliers. International customers need to rationalise their supply chain; it makes little sense for a small to medium size bookshop to trade with hundreds of suppliers with all the issues of delivery and shipping costs. The wide range of both trade and academic titles stocked by the wholesalers makes ordering from them attractive and easy, and their service levels can put publishers' own distribution to shame at times. The wholesalers are not just passive sellers in the international market place; there are a number of ways in which they can assist publishers in marketing to specific target areas overseas through buyers' notes, inserts and special offers. Publishers' export departments should be actively involved in promotional activity in what have traditionally been seen as 'UK' wholesalers.

6.3.2   UK exporters/library suppliers

It is not just the big wholesalers who are active in exporting from the UK to customers overseas. There are a number of specialist suppliers to educational, academic, professional, and library customers worldwide. In fact the visible turnover particularly for academic and STM publishers is only a proportion of what is being supplied overseas because a lot of business goes through UK-based library suppliers.

Academic and professional titles need to be very highly targeted to get to their global audience, which is exactly what the likes of Blackwells (www.blackwell.com), Coutts Information Services (www.coutts.com), Swets (www.swets.com), etc. are able to achieve with electronic and catalogue mailings to the most up-to-date contacts lists. Timely and accurate information is key to achieving good sales and that goes for what is supplied to the exporter from the publisher as it is from the exporter to the end consumer. Once again, publishers' export departments need to enter into a dialogue with those exporters which deal in the subject areas of their publishing.

7 Distribution and shipping

7.1 Getting it there

You have got your export order and
agreed the terms, now all you have
to do is get your books on a plane,
boat or truck to their destination.
This sounds simple, but logistics
is one of the biggest challenges
in export. All your hard work can
be undone by simple errors and

failures of communication between you, your UK distribution centre, your
customer and their shippers. For example, if a time-sensitive order is sent
by seafreight instead of airfreight, or is held up because of a small credit
query, it can cost you much more than the profit you would otherwise
make on the order to put things right.

7.2 Getting it right first time

The first three rules of export distribution are the same as those for chess,
'Careful, careful, careful!'.

Most problems can be avoided by being aware of what is needed in the
first place. Whenever you take or receive an order, make sure that the
following elements are clearly marked and understood. Wherever possible
most of them should be already loaded on the customer's record on your
distribution centre's database:

- The order reference.
- The titles (*Note:* including edition and binding).
- ISBN, for preference.
- Shipping instructions, including method and delivery address.
- Dues/backorder instructions.

- Special instructions – for example, enhanced discounts or packing requirements.
- Discount.
- Payment terms.

7.3   Distribution centre customer service

Your distribution centre's customer service people are at the front line of your business. Many importers will have more contact with your distributor's staff than with your own, as they are often their first point of contact for placing and chasing orders and sorting out queries. Strong regular contact with your distribution centre's customer service team is critical to the success of your export sales effort. Make an effort to get to know the team; invite them to your offices, and go and visit them to make product presentations. Give them a list of your 'gold customers', your most important stockists, distributors and retailers, to ensure that they get the best service possible.

It is well worthwhile encouraging your agents, distributors and key customers to visit your distribution centre to see your, hopefully efficient, supply chain in operation. The best distributors welcome such visits, and send their key customer service and credit control staff to London and Frankfurt book fairs to meet customers.

7.4   Handling special or urgent orders

It is worthwhile having a systematic way of handling special or urgent orders. These may include book fair orders with tricky instructions on shipping and/or documentation; urgent textbook orders, or quotations for major World Bank-funded projects. In each case, make sure that your distribution centre staff understand what and when to refer to sales management for special instructions and authorisations.

7.5   Liaison with credit control

Credit management is one of the key customer service functions. A strong link and regular communications between your credit control department, export sales team and customer service is essential.

Most distribution centres provide lists of stopped orders monthly, and flag up any substantial orders that are held up in the system because of overdue invoices on the account. Failures of communication with credit control departments are one of the major causes of customer service problems with international customers.

7.6 Shipping

Shipping costs and choice of carrier are usually decided by the customer, and it pays to follow their instructions closely. Most customers specifying sea or air freight require free freight to their forwarder. This area is fraught with problems. For example, if your customer specifies air freight for a textbook order, and your distribution centre decides knowingly or unknowingly to use seafreight, you may lose the adoption. The same may happen if you agree to release an urgent order to an account, but credit control holds it because of a small overdue payment that no-one has picked up. If you agree a particular discount for a customer without making the necessary adjustments to the customer's account record, your customer may think you are trying to cheat or renege on your agreement, and refuse to trade with you in future. As ever, accuracy, attention to detail, and communication are the keys to success.

7.7   Consolidation

Where possible, encourage your customers to use freight forwarders' consolidation services. Most established export customers ask their shippers to collect their ordered titles in reserved locations in their warehouse until an agreed weight threshold is reached. Consolidation helps reduce freight costs for your customers, and makes buying your books more profitable for them.

8 Financial issues

8.1 Direct and indirect costs

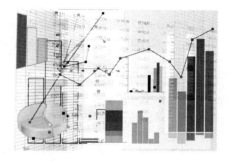

Making an export marketing plan involves a thorough examination of all the costs you will incur, including direct costs such as salaries, travel costs, book fairs and extra marketing materials, and in particular mailing. All need to be anticipated and budgeted for.

- *Commissions:* Bear in mind that typical agents' commissions are from 10 to 12.5 per cent. It is a good idea to budget for any commission bonuses you agree as well.

- *Discounts, payment periods and returns:* Discounts can be higher in export than in the UK (sometimes offset by lower export royalties), especially in emerging markets such as Eastern Europe and Asia. Discounts should be set by territory, not by product lines. It is a good idea to simplify complex UK discount structures into, say, hardback and paperback terms. Short discounts on special products such as big reference works may not be workable in some markets.

- *Promotion material production:* Export may require extra selling materials, in particular sales kits for representatives, and any illustrated selling materials can substantially increase your costs.

- *Mailing:* Mailing can be expensive, especially if you use mailing houses. For deliveries it is best to use the customer's shipper, if they allow that.

- *Returns and dead stock provision:* Bear in mind that if you are making consignment stock arrangements with distributors, or allowing returns, your finance director should make provision for these eventualities. In the case of trade titles and textbooks, many publishers accept either returns of covers or certificated returns, i.e., third-party authorisation that stock has been destroyed, to avoid the cost of physically returning dead stock.

- *Travel and entertainment:* Ideally, the year's travel plans should be mapped out in advance, preferably at budget time, and costs projected accordingly.

- *Exhibitions and sales conferences:* Frankfurt and London book fairs are becoming the essential export forums now, and neither is particularly cheap to attend. Do not forget that you may qualify for a UK Trade & Investment subsidy. If you are planning an international sales conference, you will need to apportion enough budget to give your guests a reasonable time. Many of them will have attended hundreds of sales conferences in their time, so you will have to do something special for them to remember yours.

- *Exchange rate risks:* Given that most export sales transactions are based on long-ish credit periods, fluctuating world currency markets present a risk to exporting publishers if billing in currencies other than Sterling. However, your customers' financial situation may become difficult even with a small percentage change in rates, and that can put pressure on their or your position. If billing in foreign currency, consider buying currency forward (i.e., in advance), and watch exchange rate projections carefully.

8.2   Credit control

It is quite natural that a favourite question of financial directors confronted with export opportunities is, 'Will we get paid?' After all, plenty of publishers have not in the past. Although the credit environment in international markets is probably better today than ever before, there is always a risk of your customers getting into trouble with their cash flow, because of over-enthusiastic stock holding or macro-economic circumstances.

At worst, poor and conservative credit control can be the death of your export effort. There is no point spending money travelling to a territory when all the orders are held up on your return. At best, an intelligent, entrepreneurial credit controller will join you in understanding the needs of challenging markets, and work out the best way to approach them.

The usual credit control requirements on new accounts includes the following:

- **References:** Two or three publishers already trading with the account, plus the customer's bank reference
- **Credit limits:** Usually based on what analogous publishers are giving them.

8.3   Controlling risk

Controlling risk in export credit management can be done by buying credit insurance such as ECGD (www.ecgd.gov.uk). Exchange rate fluctuations can be protected against by buying forward currencies. Most important of all is regular contact between your sales people, agents and distribution centre to pick up any problems early.

Appendices

Appendix 1: Export statistics

A1.1 UK publishers' exports of physical books by sector and region 2006-2010

	TOTAL	Europe	Mid East/ N Africa	Africa Sub-Sahara	E & S Asia	Australasia	North America	Other Americas	Unspecified
FICTION									
	£m	£m	£m	£m	£m	£m	£m	£m	£m
2006	124	48	3	8	10	41	13	1	*
2007	140	55	3	9	12	47	14	1	*
2008	142	51	3	9	12	53	14	1	*
2009	158	58	3	9	13	58	15	1	*
2010	158	59	3	10	14	54	17	1	*
% change in sales									
2009/10	-0.3	+1.3	+3.1	+3.0	+5.6	-7.4	+12.1	+28.0	-44.4
2006/10	+27.0	+21.8	+31.4	+17.6	+35.4	+31.9	+31.4	+16.6	-50.9
NON-FICTION/REFERENCE									
	£m	£m	£m	£m	£m	£m	£m	£m	£m
2006	188	82	9	14	23	34	22	4	1
2007	198	80	10	21	27	35	22	4	1
2008	204	81	12	15	27	41	23	5	2
2009	200	79	12	14	29	37	24	3	2
2010	210	82	13	15	29	39	26	3	2
% change in sales									
2009/10	+5.1	+4.4	+13.1	+7.7	-0.9	+6.2	+7.5	+2.1	+8.6
2006/10	+12.1	+0.4	+55.4	+11.3	+22.8	+16.6	+19.4	-5.7	

	TOTAL	Europe	Mid East/ N Africa	Africa Sub-Sahara	E & S Asia	Australasia	North America	Other Americas	Unspecified

CHILDREN'S

	£m	£m	£m	£m	£m	£m	£m	£m	£m
2006	71	18	4	6	14	18	8	3	*
2007	121	46	6	13	21	27	8	2	*
2008	87	24	6	7	17	25	6	2	*
2009	95	27	6	8	17	28	8	2	*
2010	88	22	6	10	18	23	8	2	*

% change in sales

2009/10	-7.2	-16.9	-4.7	+25.8	+1.9	-18.2	+3.5	+21.8	-17.2
2006/10	+24.8	+23.0	+33.7	+69.5	+23.1	+28.7	+7.9	-31.2	-81.7

SCHOOL/ELT

	£m	£m	£m	£m	£m	£m	£m	£m	£m
2006	255	116	30	20	38	2	9	39	*
2007	275	131	31	23	40	2	10	39	*
2008	305	138	36	38	39	2	10	41	*
2009	304	138	43	23	42	2	9	46	*
2010	308	134	49	25	39	3	7	51	*

% change in sales

2009/10	+1.2	-3.2	+14.1	+8.2	-7.3	+29.8	-25.8	+10.7	-31.1
2006/10	+20.7	+15.4	+63.4	+22.4	+2.0	+38.6	-23.5	+30.8	-77.5

ACADEMIC /PROFESSIONAL

	£m	£m	£m	£m	£m	£m	£m	£m	£m
2006	386	154	49	30	63	11	70	4	5
2007	397	157	54	32	65	11	69	4	4
2008	423	164	60	35	70	12	76	3	4
2009	445	170	66	45	74	12	71	2	4
2010	490	173	77	53	83	13	84	3	5

% change in sales

2009/10	+10.1	+1.9	+16.8	+16.4	+11.3	+7.9	+18.0	+19.3	+11.2
2006/10	+26.8	+12.6	+57.9	+77.2	+30.6	+11.2	+19.6	-30.1	-8.0

	TOTAL	Europe	Mid East/ N Africa	Africa Sub-Sahara	E & S Asia	Australasia	North America	Other Americas	Unspecified
TOTAL EXPORTS									
	£m	£m	£m	£m	£m	£m	£m	£m	£m
2006	1024	418	94	78	150	106	122	50	7
2007	1132	468	103	97	165	121	122	50	5
2008	1162	458	118	104	164	132	128	51	6
2009	1203	472	130	100	176	137	128	54	6
2010	1254	470	148	112	182	132	143	60	7
% change in sales									
2009/10	+4.3	-0.3	+14.2	+12.7	+3.5	-4.0	+11.2	+11.0	+7.8
2006/10	+22.5	+12.5	+57.6	+44.4	+21.7	+24.4	+16.9	+19.9	+4.6

NB (1): Percentage changes calcuated before rounding.

NB (2): The above figures related to physical book exports only.

Source: PA Statistics Yearbook 2010, (c) The Publishers Association 2011

A1.2   BIS value of book exports (and re-exports) by country 2008-2010

The Department of Business, Innovation and Skills (BIS) Statistics Directorate figures on the value of book exports is based on HM Revenue and Customs data and as such includes brochures and similar printed matter based on the following Standard Industrial Classification Codes (SITC):

- 89212: Children's picture, drawing or colouring books.
- 89213: Printed Maps and Charts in Book Form.
- 89214: Maps & hydrographic or similar charts of all kinds (including globes), printed, not in book form.
- 89215: Printed books, brochures, leaflets similar printed matter in single sheets, folded or not (excluding advertising) .
- 89216:Dictionaries & encyclopaedias and serial instalments thereof not in single sheets.
- 89219: Other books, brochures and similar printed matter, not in single sheet (not including advertising materials).

The figures also include the re-export of books and therefore over-estimate the export sales however they are useful for trends. It is worth noting that the entrepots such as Singapore and Dubai may distort the figures. For further information on HM Revenue & Customs' trade statistics, visit the HMRC's UKtradeinfo website: (www.uktradeinfo.com).

Value of book exports (and re-exports) by country 2008-2010

Ranked by 2010	2008 Exports £ sterling	2009 Exports £ sterling	2010 Exports £ sterling	% Change 2009/10
UNITED STATES	172,343,218	167,858,403	181,672,181	8.2
GERMANY	120,006,307	137,813,063	140,450,884	1.9
IRISH REPUBLIC	160,529,890	145,169,628	136,864,432	-5.7
AUSTRALIA	86,587,229	100,359,700	101,545,141	1.2
NETHERLANDS	97,769,061	97,222,922	72,370,979	-25.6
FRANCE	72,554,581	68,655,172	67,723,057	-1.4
SOUTH AFRICA	47,854,767	58,224,420	62,839,558	7.9
SPAIN	59,748,846	62,503,838	58,795,414	-5.9
SINGAPORE	50,553,169	47,418,580	49,533,329	4.5
ITALY	48,875,532	49,825,384	47,141,900	-5.4
JAPAN	47,129,635	60,192,192	46,430,260	-22.9
SWEDEN	38,018,322	39,502,366	46,306,742	17.2
BELGIUM	32,254,415	37,864,146	37,900,725	0.1
INDIA	23,881,063	26,619,073	34,281,623	28.8
CANADA	25,014,646	29,846,841	33,612,286	12.6
CHINA	15,314,768	22,156,132	33,299,857	50.3
UAE	26,309,558	25,595,593	31,567,622	23.3
DENMARK	29,831,975	29,718,907	26,257,667	-11.6
NORWAY	26,454,475	27,116,314	25,909,066	-4.5
GREECE	33,132,380	34,129,062	25,797,164	-24.4
POLAND	22,717,800	25,013,510	24,390,513	-2.5
SWITZERLAND	24,281,847	22,841,793	20,670,346	-9.5
HONG KONG	15,312,871	16,800,442	19,613,836	16.7
SAUDI ARABIA	12,531,863	16,897,361	19,299,687	14.2
NEW ZEALAND	10,411,481	13,102,409	16,101,987	22.9
SOUTH KOREA	12,439,119	14,657,205	16,024,021	9.3
AUSTRIA	8,060,521	7,808,827	14,895,079	90.7
TURKEY	12,456,157	12,873,340	14,873,789	15.5
BRAZIL	10,634,281	11,152,808	14,833,651	33

The Publishers Association

Ranked by 2010	2008 Exports £ sterling	2009 Exports £ sterling	2010 Exports £ sterling	% Change 2009/10
RUSSIA	15,345,369	13,590,290	14,252,102	4.9
FINLAND	13,187,380	13,688,575	12,521,464	-8.5
PORTUGAL	10,907,751	12,340,536	10,761,196	-12.8
EGYPT	8,252,933	11,131,036	10,582,700	-4.9
CZECH REPUBLIC	11,469,290	9,759,428	9,416,943	-3.5
TAIWAN	8,688,692	8,815,699	9,343,603	6
IRAN	8,695,651	7,410,374	9,305,793	25.6
NIGERIA	6,835,981	8,768,113	8,898,304	1.5
HUNGARY	8,058,440	7,010,990	6,846,077	-2.4
KENYA	5,797,831	5,289,496	6,571,744	24.2
SLOVENIA	5,472,689	6,497,360	6,388,638	-1.7
MALTA	5,157,592	5,877,252	6,362,561	8.3
MALAYSIA	4,881,679	6,021,556	6,272,587	4.2
MEXICO	3,737,796	3,626,478	5,915,077	63.1
THAILAND	5,059,949	3,711,890	5,354,442	44.3
LEBANON	4,082,519	4,812,518	5,285,472	9.8
JAMAICA	5,529,714	4,890,992	4,985,155	1.9
JORDAN	4,258,142	4,941,989	4,933,939	-0.2
SLOVAKIA	2,646,423	3,357,293	4,753,487	41.6
CYPRUS	4,759,218	5,175,459	4,646,179	-10.2
LUXEMBOURG	1,729,227	1,835,143	4,460,813	143.1
ISRAEL	4,702,824	4,946,131	4,250,276	-14.1
TRINIDAD &TOBAGO	4,996,278	4,751,674	3,923,524	-17.4
ARGENTINA	4,927,763	2,149,147	3,781,263	75.9
BAHRAIN	2,680,815	3,515,404	3,750,516	6.7
QATAR	2,918,305	3,289,209	3,598,490	9.4
KUWAIT	2,461,801	3,770,673	3,514,274	-6.8
ROMANIA	4,122,623	3,784,149	3,443,977	-9
PAKISTAN	2,147,337	1,580,625	3,000,847	89.9
GHANA	3,404,672	3,169,546	2,802,176	-11.6
CROATIA	3,903,486	3,341,515	2,794,310	-16.4
OMAN	2,655,066	2,891,824	2,738,610	-5.3
SERBIA	2,902,888	3,649,239	2,716,336	-25.6
UKRAINE	1,760,161	2,779,103	2,635,854	-5.2
PANAMA	254,316	251,003	2,428,017	867.3

Ranked by 2010	2008 Exports £ sterling	2009 Exports £ sterling	2010 Exports £ sterling	% Change 2009/10
MOROCCO	1,636,099	2,168,674	2,402,997	10.8
BULGARIA	2,997,868	2,720,950	2,386,991	-12.3
PERU	2,445,943	2,047,497	2,373,672	15.9
ICELAND	2,286,878	1,788,132	2,317,022	29.6
PHILIPPINES	2,223,202	2,426,423	2,285,041	-5.8
SYRIA	2,187,877	4,570,464	2,251,063	-50.7
ZAMBIA	1,302,610	2,132,925	2,246,849	5.3
ETHIOPIA	1,563,135	1,669,796	2,073,113	24.2
KAZAKHSTAN	1,073,894	1,238,697	2,014,463	62.6
COLOMBIA	1,017,552	1,312,071	1,687,100	28.6
BARBADOS	1,775,785	1,857,338	1,654,598	-10.9
UGANDA	1,621,355	1,171,652	1,631,279	39.2
SRI LANKA	1,224,758	1,224,310	1,514,125	23.7
TANZANIA	1,181,799	1,247,945	1,499,564	20.2
SUDAN	371,923	752,134	1,402,261	86.4
CHILE	2,195,061	1,163,052	1,360,101	16.9
MAURITIUS	957,371	1,172,751	1,339,808	14.2
ESTONIA	1,761,225	1,440,844	1,323,424	-8.1
YEMEN	756,582	1,599,478	1,162,865	-27.3
LITHUANIA	1,775,256	1,183,300	1,110,653	-6.1
LATVIA	1,617,491	1,267,735	995,366	-21.5
VIETNAM	783,327	1,213,708	975,714	-19.6
BAHAMAS	1,037,217	1,096,853	971,855	-11.4
MALAWI	1,848,425	1,499,552	927,450	-38.2
LIBYA	433,752	2,412,611	909,410	-62.3
GIBRALTAR	686,480	769,788	844,179	9.7
ALGERIA	440,159	741,878	804,100	8.4
RWANDA	208,691	466,221	719,041	54.2
AFGHANISTAN	194,658	856,275	712,519	-16.8
INDONESIA	477,719	450,304	700,446	55.5
ECUADOR	692,151	606,055	691,549	14.1
ST LUCIA	700,204	488,142	682,939	39.9
ANTIGUA:BARBUDA	766,024	844,979	641,204	-24.1
ANGOLA	574,959	660,083	590,966	-10.5
IRAQ	169,063	512,189	533,573	4.2

Ranked by 2010	2008 Exports £ sterling	2009 Exports £ sterling	2010 Exports £ sterling	% Change 2009/10
URUGUAY	800,441	1,159,827	523,734	-54.8
ZIMBABWE	151,700	340,785	510,213	49.7
GEORGIA	362,170	452,032	498,051	10.2
BOTSWANA	599,556	512,209	494,047	-3.5
TUNISIA	506,079	551,543	483,819	-12.3
CONGO (REPUBLIC)	142,275	353,411	472,688	33.8
BOSNIA & HERZ.	302,243	443,257	470,943	6.2
LIBERIA	51,507	59,742	449,754	652.8
VENEZUELA	179,497	545,429	447,060	-18
CAYMAN ISLANDS	487,257	341,435	436,044	27.7
MONTENEGRO	252,492	3,961	420,583	10,518.10
ST VINCENT	502,018	668,252	412,831	-38.2
BR VIRGIN IS	141,054	236,890	404,725	70.8
GRENADA	733,991	643,259	398,484	-38.1
FYR MACEDONIA	601,426	625,090	395,598	-36.7
ALBANIA	177,772	298,790	340,348	13.9
DOMINICA	462,411	303,711	332,873	9.6
NAMIBIA	47,665	173,023	323,695	87.1
MACAO	6,128	4,983	319,182	6,305.40
BRUNEI	188,412	375,920	292,960	-22.1
BELIZE	856,622	666,426	290,116	-56.5
BURUNDI	11,194	54,030	282,460	422.8
GAMBIA	505,258	417,141	258,406	-38.1
GUYANA	526,041	531,834	251,144	-52.8
ARMENIA	236,385	64,534	249,414	286.5
BELARUS	381,487	214,639	245,224	14.2
CAMEROON	304,285	255,677	231,395	-9.5
ST KITTS & NEVIS	149,032	178,924	229,662	28.4
BERMUDA	109,924	230,276	224,876	-2.3
CUBA	213,483	173,940	220,994	27.1
PARAGUAY	171,840	51,667	194,701	276.8
MALDIVES	269,798	285,711	193,936	-32.1
TOGO	124,303	194,538	189,437	-2.6
SIERRA LEONE	24,837	74,318	188,811	154.1
COSTA RICA	125,652	94,468	183,372	94.1

Ranked by 2010	2008 Exports £ sterling	2009 Exports £ sterling	2010 Exports £ sterling	% Change 2009/10
ERITREA	77,302	402,563	162,300	-59.7
AZERBAIJAN	214,060	131,095	161,111	22.9
SEYCHELLES	116,638	94,113	157,711	67.6
MAURITANIA	3,716	293,566	156,742	-46.6
SENEGAL	129,239	54,390	150,138	176
BANGLADESH	122,938	110,642	123,817	11.9
TURKS & CAICOS	41,513	181,809	118,475	-34.8
UZBEKISTAN	666,396	621,967	115,922	-81.4
BOLIVIA	182,252	215,930	97,288	-54.9
CAMBODIA	103,561	62,468	96,676	54.8
MOLDOVA	64,945	331,070	86,186	-74
BENIN	21,867	86,007	82,841	-3.7
MADAGASCAR	11,009	23,062	78,924	242.2
LAOS	6,674	4,583	69,348	1,413.20
FALKLAND ISLANDS	58,169	73,594	67,816	-7.9
MOZAMBIQUE	91,635	66,300	66,823	0.8
ANGUILLA	60,321	60,784	61,139	0.6
KOSOVO	43,525	25,933	60,518	133.4
CHAD	5,100	6,527	58,912	802.6
DOMINICAN REP	51,398	92,704	50,914	-45.1
GUINEA-BISSAU	0	0	48,947	n/a
NL ANTILLES	.n/a	92,708	48,417	-47.8
GUINEA	14,358	14,125	41,411	193.2
SAN MARINO	9,221	90,383	39,174	-56.7
BURMA	6,786	5,070	35,888	607.9
EL SALVADOR	5,148	26,650	31,226	17.2
CONGO (DEM. REP)	422,388	403,987	30,194	-92.5
FIJI	13,206	6,913	28,326	309.7
HAITI	2,779	0	27,677	n/a
IVORY COAST	450,426	112,777	27,146	-75.9
BURKINA	24,916	86,901	26,717	-69.3
EQUAT GUINEA	23,376	28,941	26,517	-8.4
TIMOR-LESTE	0	19,968	23,215	16.3
NEPAL	16,273	11,817	19,463	64.7
SAMOA	0	3,778	18,914	400.6

Ranked by 2010	2008 Exports £ sterling	2009 Exports £ sterling	2010 Exports £ sterling	% Change 2009/10
MONGOLIA	45,664	32,496	15,342	-52.8
SOMALIA	3,448	2,057	14,762	617.6
PAPUA NEW GUINEA	11,568	12,165	13,238	8.8
TAJIKISTAN	1,249	10,940	13,174	20.4
FAROE ISLANDS	11,160	726	12,402	1,608.30
GABON	377,881	34,762	10,687	-69.3
HONDURAS	15,853	7,241	9,621	32.9
SURINAM	5,518	10,435	7,860	-24.7
TURKMENISTAN	59,676	1,478	7,794	427.3
US VIRGIN IS	19,980	44,867	7,730	-82.8
LESOTHO	0	100,389	7,579	-92.5
MONTSERRAT	15,987	11,597	6,396	-44.8
DJIBOUTI	9,921	100,200	6,362	-93.7
NEW CALEDONIA	3,686	5,380	6,313	17.3
MARSHALL ISLANDS	19,494	0	5,331	n/a
FRENCH POLYNESIA	39,188	27,842	4,998	-82
NICARAGUA	820	24,971	4,959	-80.1
GREENLAND	0	0	4,733	n/a
GUATEMALA	16,148	8,927	4,697	-47.4
CAPE VERDE	887	800	4,115	414.4
CENT AFR REP	1,508	0	3,987	n/a
CEUTA	4,040	2,284	3,945	72.7
SWAZILAND	2,404	49,132	3,115	-93.7
MALI	14,388	6,414	2,666	-58.4
LIECHTENSTEIN	1,760,534	7,898	2,250	-71.5
SOLOMON ISLANDS	2,582	3,478	1,533	-55.9
ARUBA	1,993	866	1,489	71.9
SOUTH GEORGIA IS	0	3,580	1,485	-58.5
ANDORRA	23,799	8,583	1,406	-83.6
KYRGYZ REPUBLIC	772,032	612,833	1,228	-99.8
KIRIBATI	2,757	0	953	n/a
ST HELENA	854	2,000	889	-55.6
GUAM	1,721	1,790	741	-58.6
BHUTAN	19,060	0	608	n/a

Appendix 2: Useful resources for digital market information

2.1   Digital statistics

(NB: Remember to check the websites of local trade associations.)

The Publishers Association: Through its annual statistics yearbook the PA provides a digital section showing UK publishers' total sales of digital products. Export sales are not shown separately as yet but it does include estimates of total sales by the following sectors: Consumer, Consumer Reference, School/ELT, and Academic/Professional. www.publishers.org.uk

The International Digital Publishing Forum (IDPF): In conjunction with the Association of American Publishers (AAP), the IDPF collects quarterly US trade retail e-book sales. http://idpf.org/about-us/industry-statistics

Börsenverein des Deutschen Buchhandels e.V & GfK Panel: The German Book Publishers and Booksellers Association with GFK Panel have recently conducted a study on the E-book market in Germany. www.boersenblatt.net/437542/template/bb_tpl_branchenstudien/

PricewaterhouseCoopers: In 2010 PWC published a report *Turning the Page: The Future of ebooks* which looks at market developments in the UK, USA, Germany and the Netherlands from both the publishing side and the consumer side. www.pwc.com/en_GX/gx/entertainment-media/pdf/eBooks-Trends-Developments.pdf

The Bookseller: Philip Jones of *The Bookseller* recently published an edited version of the IPA members' responses to questions on their developing e-book markets. The article "Global e-book market" dated 14 March 2011 included estimates of export markets for Germany, Japan, South Korea, Netherlands ,South Africa, Spain, Italy, and the USA. www.thebookseller.com/feature/digital-focus-global-e-book-market.html

Accenture: Accenture published its *2011 Consumer Electronics Products and Services Usage Report - Finding Growth: Emergence of a New Consumer Technology Paradigm.* The aim of this research was to help consumer technology executives better understand the purchase and use of consumer technologies among key generations and to gain deeper insights into global differences. The countries within the survey were: USA, Japan, Germany, France, Brazil, Russia, India and China. https://microsite.accenture.com/landing_pages/EHT/Documents/ Accenture_GlobalConsumerTech_2011.pdfreferred Letter

2.2   VAT

International Publishers Association & PricewaterhouseCooper: The IPA & PWC conduct an annual global survey on VAT/ GST/Sales Tax Rates on books and electronic publications. www.internationalpublishers.org/index.php/-industry-policy/vat/ipa-vat-annual-survey.

Appendix 3: Export agents

The following is a selective listing of agents (freelance export sales representatives worldwide). For reasons of space, it is not fully comprehensive, it does not include representatives for Ireland or the US, and comes with no particular recommendation.

A3.1 World

Gunnar Lie & Associates Ltd
Linkside, New Malden
Surrey KT3 4LA
UK
Tel: + 44 (0)20 8605 1097
Fax: + 44 (0) 20 8605 1098
Email: gunnar@gunnarlie.com
Sales territories: Europe, Middle East,
Asia, Africa (inc South Africa), Caribbean &
South America

Torpedo Global Sales Network
Website: www.torpedo-global.com
Federation of experienced independent
publishers' sales agencies (listed in
sections below)
Sales territories: World

A3.2 Europe

Angell Eurosales
The Old Whaling House
The Walls
Berwick-upon-Tweed TD15 1HP
UK
Contact: Gill Angell
Tel: +44 (0) 1289 332934
Fax: + 44 (0) 1289 332935
Email: info@angelleurosales.com
Sales territories: Europe
Specialisation: Trade & Academic

Anglo Nordic Books Ltd
15 Marshall Road
Godalming
Surrey GU7 3AS
UK
Contact: Peter A. Barrows
Tel: +44 (0) 1483 422395
Fax: + 44 (0) 1483 423444
Email: pb@anglonordicbooks.com
Sales territories: Scandinavia
Specialisation: Illustrated Non-fiction,
Classic Fiction

Bill Bailey Publishers' Representatives
16 Devon Square
Newton Abbot
Devon TQ12 2HR
UK
Contact: Bill Bailey
Tel: +44 (0) 1626 331079
Fax: + 44 (0) 1626 331 080
Email: info@billbaileypubreps.co.uk
Sales territories: Europe
Specialisation: All subjects

Bookport Associates
Via Luigi Salma 7
20094 Corsico (MI)
Italy
Contact: Joe Portelli
Tel: +39 2 4510 3601
Fax: +39 2 4510 6426
Email: bookport.associates@libero.it
Sales territories: Southern European
region which include: Italy, Spain,
Gibraltar, Portugal, Greece, Cyprus, Malta,
Slovenia, Croatia, Bosnia & Serbia
Specialisation: Trade

Books For Europe
CP 196
CH 6908 Massagno
Switzerland
Contact: Mr Juliusz Komarnicki, Managing
Director
Tel: +41 91 967 1539
Fax: +41 91 966 7865
Email: juliusz.komarnicki@bluewin.ch
Website: www.booksforeurope.com
Sales territories: Austria, France &
Switzerland
Specialisation: All subjects

Also at:

Vosberger Weg 22
8181 JH Heerde
Netherlands
Contact: Robbert Pleysier
Tel: +31 578 696 596
Fax: +31 578 696 798
Email: rjpleysier.bfe@planet.nl
Sales territories: Benelux & Germany
Specialisation: All subjects

Also at:

Borgediget, 13, st
4000 Roskilde
Denmark
Contact: Pernille Larsen
Tel: +45 46 36 02 99
Fax: +45 46 36 62 99
Mobile: +45 2371 4623
Email: p-larsen@mail.tele.dk
Sales territories: Scandinavia
Specialisation: All subjects

Also at:

Books For Eastern Europe
Tinodi u. 31
1047 Budapest
Hungary
Contact: Dr Laszlo Horvath
Tel: +36 1 370 3614
Fax: + 36 1 379 5842
Email: laszlo@laszlo-horvath.hu
Sales territories: Central & Eastern Europe
Specialisation: All subjects

Also at:

Via Guelfa 91
50129 Firenze
Italy
Contact: Sandro Salucci
Tel/Fax: +39 055 284 612
Mobile: +39 335 242 069
Email: sandro.salucci@libero.it
Sales territories: Greece, Italy, Spain,
Portugal, Gibraltar, Croatia, & Slovenia
Specialisation: All subjects

C.L.B. Marketing Services
PO Box 934
H-1244 Budapest
Hungary
Contact: Csaba & Jackie Lengyel de
Bagota
Tel/Fax: +36 1 340 5213
Email: clb@matavnet.hu
Sales territories: Macedonia, Serbia,
Croatia, Montenegro, Bosnia-
Herzegovenia, Hungary, Czech Republic,
Poland, Slovakia, Slovenia

Colin Flint Limited
26 Harvey Goodwin Avenue
Cambridge CM4 3EU
UK
Contact: Ben Greig
Tel & Fax: +44 (0) 1223 565 052
Email: ben.greig@dial.pipex.com
Sales territories: Denmark, Finland,
Iceland, Norway, & Sweden
Specialisation: Academic

Consul Books
Kerkpad 18
1261 TJ Blaricum
The Netherlands
Contact: Alma van Zaane
Tel: +31 (0)35 531 2609
Fax: +31 (0)35 538 2369
Email: consulbooks@wxs.nl
Sales territories: The Netherlands
Specialisation: All subjects

Continental Contacts
Diederik van Altenastraat 12
5095 AP Hooge Mierde
The Netherlands
Contact: Mr Roy de Boo
Tel: +31 13 509 6033
Fax: +31 13 509 6034
Email: r.w.l.de.boo@hetnet.nl
Sales territories: Belgium, Germany, & The
Netherlands
Specialisation: Academic

David Towle International
Lagebergsvagen 15
SE – 136 67 Haninge
Stockholm
Sweden
Contact: Mr David Towle
Tel: +46 8 777 3962
Fax: +46 8 777 1470
Email: david@dti.a.se
Sales territories: Denmark, Estonia,
Finland, Iceland, Latvia, Lithuania, Norway,
& Sweden
Specialisation: Academic

Durnell Marketing Limited
2 Linden Close
Tunbridge Wells
Kent TN4 8HH
UK
Contact: Andrew Durnell
Tel: +44 (0) 1892 544272
Fax: +44 (0) 1892 511152
Email: mail@durnell.co.uk
Sales territories: Europe
Specialisation: Academic, Professional, Reference and Trade

European Marketing Services
55 Overhill Road
Dulwich
London SE22 OPQ
UK
Contact: Anselm Robinson
Tel: +44 (0) 20 8516 5433
Fax: +44 (0) 20 8516 5434
Email: anselm.robinson@gmail.com
Sales territories: Austria, Belgium, France, Germany, Netherlands & Switzerland
Specialisation: Trade

Ewa Ledóchowicz
ul. Tuwima 6
05-520 Konstancin-Jeziorna
near Warsaw
Poland
Contact: Ewa Ledóchowicz
Tel: +48 22 754 1764
Fax: +48 22 756 4572
Email: ewa@adtv.pl
Sales territories: Croatia, Czech Republic, Estonia, Hungary, Poland, Romania, Slovak Republic, & Slovenia
Specialisation: Trade and Academic

HRA
5 Voluntary Place
Wanstead
London E11 2RP
UK
Contact: Chris Humphrys
Tel: +44 (0) 20 8530 5028
Fax: +44 (0) 20 8530 7870
Email: humph4HRA@gmail.com
Sales territories: Spain & Portugal
Specialisation: Trade, Academic

Iberian Book Services
Sector Islas, Bloque, 12, 1B
Madrid
28760 Tres Cantos
Spain
Contact: Peter Prout
Tel: +34 91 803 49 18
Fax: +34 91 803 59 36
Email: pprout@telefonica.net
Sales territories: Spain, Portugal, Gibraltar
Specialisation: Trade

IMA
14 York Rise
London NW5 1ST
UK
Contact: Tony Moggach
Tel:+44 (0) 20 7267 8054
Fax: +44 (0) 20 7485 8463
Email: ima@moggach.demon.co.uk
Sales territories: Eastern Europe & Russia
Specialisation: Trade

J&L Watt Publishing Consultants
26 Temple Street
Oxford
OX4 1JS
UK
Tel: +44 (0)1865 202829
Fax: +44 (0)1865 202830
Email: james@jlwatt.co.uk
Sales territories: Cyprus, Malta, & Greece
Specialisation: Academic

JN Publishers' Representative
Jomsborgvej 22
DK 3650 Olstykke
Denmark
Contact: Jan Norbye
Tel: +45 47 17 40 48
Sales territory: Scandinavia
Specialisation: Academic

Marcello s.a.s
Via Belzoni 12
35121 Padova
Italy
Contact: Mr Flavio Marcello
Tel: +39 49 836 0671
Fax: +39 49 878 6759
Email: marcello@marvcellosas.it
Sales territories: France, Italy, Portugal, & Spain
Specialisation: Academic

Mare Nostrum Publishing Consultants
Via Tiburtina Antica 13
Interno 11b
00185 Roma
Italy
Contact: David Pickering
Tel:+39 348 318 3884
Email: davidpickering@mare-nostrum.co.uk
Sales territories: France & Italy
Specialisation: Academic and Professional

Also at :

Condessa de Chinchon 25, Chalet 68
28660 Boadilla del Monte
Madrid
Spain
Contact: Cristina de Lara Ruiz
Tel/Fax: +34 91 633 6665
Email: christinadelara@mare-nostrum.co.uk
Sales territories: Spain & Portugal

Marek Lewinson
Bohaterewicza 3/45
03-982 Warsaw
Poland
Tel/Fax:+48 22 671 4819
Mobile: +48 602 707037
Email: mlewinso@it.com.pl
Sales territories: Eastern Europe
Specialisation: Academic

McNeish Publishing International
3 Coastguard Cottages
Toot Rock, Pett Level
East Sussex TN35 4EW
UK
Contact: Katie McNeish
Tel: + 44 (0) 1424 813124
Fax: + 44 (0) 1424 813126
Email: kt@globescribe.demon.co.uk
Sales territories: Scandinavia & Italy
Specialisation: Trade

Michael Geoghegan
14 Frognal Gardens
London NW3 6UX
UK
Tel: +44 (0) 20 7435 1662
Fax: +44 (0) 20 7435 0180
Mobile: +44 (0) 7712 189 415
Email: michael@geoghegan.me.uk
Sales territories: Belgium, France,
Netherlands, Germany, Austria,
Switzerland, Poland, Hungary, Czech
Republic, Slovakia, Croatia, & Slovenia.
Specialisation: Trade

Netwerk Academic Book Agency
P.O. Box 33228
2005 EE Rotterdam
The Netherlands
Contact: Frank Janssen
Tel: +3110 461 3868
Fax: +3110 461 4645
Email: info@netwerkaba.com
Website: www.netwerkaba.com
Sales territories: Belgium, Luxembourg &,
The Netherlands
Specialisation: Academic & Bookshops

Penny Padovani
56 Rosebank
Holyport Road
London SW6 6LH
UK
Tel/Fax: +44 (0)20 7381 3936
Email: padovanibooks@compuserve.com
Sales territories: Greece & Italy
Specialisation: All areas

Also at:

Jenny Padovani
Tel: +34 637 027 587
Email: jenny@padovanibooks.com
Sales territories: Portugal & Spain
Specialisation: All areas

Peter Ward Book Exports
Unit 3, Taylors Yard
67 Alderbook Road
London SW12 8AD
UK
Contact: Richard and Peter Ward
Tel: +44 (0)20 8772 3300
Fax: +44 (0)20 8772 3309
Email: richard@pwbx.com
Sales territories: Turkey, Cyprus, & Malta
Specialisation: Trade

P.S. Publishers' Services
Zeigenhainer Straße 169
D-60433 Frankfurt
Germany
Contact: Gabi Kern
Tel: +49 69 510694
Fax: +49 69 510695
Email: Gabriele.Kern@publishersservices.de
Sales territories: Austria, Germany, & Switzerland
Specialisation: Trade

SHS Publishers' Consultants and Representatives
Am Kanal 25
D-16515 Oranienburg
Germany
Contact: Bernd Feldmann
Tel: +49-3301 20 57 75
Fax: +49-3301 20 57 82
Email: BFeldmann@snafu.de
Website: www.shs-feldmann.de
Sales territories: Germany, Austria, Switzerland

Ted Dougherty
72 Hadley St
London NW1 8TA
UK
Tel: +44 (0) 20 7482 2439
Fax: +44 (0) 20 7267 9310
Email: ted.dougherty@blueyonder.co.uk
Sales territories: Europe
Specialisation: Trade

Van de Bilt Sales & Marketing Ltd
Forgandenny
High Wych
Sawbridgeworth
Herts CM21 0HX
UK
Contact: Theo van de Bilt
Tel/Fax: +44 (0) 1279 725468
Mobile: +44 (0) 7956 320574
Email: theo@vandebilt.co.uk
Sales territories: Netherlands, Belgium, Luxembourg, & occasionally Scandinavia
Specialisation: Academic

A3.3 Middle East

Avicenna Partnership Ltd
PO Box 484
Oxford OX2 9WQ
UK
Contact: Bill Kennedy
Tel: +44 (0)7802 244 457
Email: bill.kennedy@BTInternet.com
Sales territory: Middle East
Contact: Claire de Gruchy
Tel: +44 (0)7771 887 843
Email: claire_degruchy@yahoo.co.uk
Sales territories: North Africa & South East Europe

IPR International Publishers Representatives
PO Box 25731, 1311 Nicosia
Cyprus
Contact: David Atiyah
Tel: +357 22 872 355
Fax: +357 22 872 359
Email: iprschl@spidernet.com.cy
Sales territories: Middle East & North Africa, Greece, Cyprus, & Turkey
Specialisation: Academic

International Publishing Services
P O Box 27533, Dubai
United Arab Emirates
Contact: Zoe Kaviani/Faris Bukhari
Tel: +971 4 282 8801
Fax: +971 4 282 8804
Email: ipsgroup@emirates.net.ae
Website: www.ipsme.com
Sales territories: Bahrain, Iran, Jordan, Kuwait, Lebanon, Oman, Qatar, Saudi Arabia, Syria, The United Emirates, Turkey, & Yemen
Specialisation: Academic, Trade

Also at:

Vijeh Nashr Company
International Books & Journals Services
No. 1, Havapeymaee Alley
Nejatollahi St, Teheran 15996
Iran
Tel: +98 21 8891 0429
Fax: +98 21 8891 0430
Email: info@vijehnashr.com
Sales territory: Iran
Specialisation: Academic

J&L Watt Publishing Consultants
26 Temple Street
Oxford OX4 1JS
UK
Tel: 44 (0)1865 202829
Fax: 44 (0)1865 202830
Email: james@jlwatt.co.uk
Sales territories: Middle East
Specialisation: Academic

Peter Ward Book Exports
Unit 3, Taylors Yard
67 Alderbook Road
London SW12 8AD
UK
Contact: Richard and Peter Ward
Tel: +44 (0)20 8772 3300
Fax: +44 (0)20 8772 3309
Email: richard@pwbx.com
Sales territories: Turkey, Cyprus, & Malta
Specialisation: Trade

Publishers International Marketing
Polfages
11420 Villautou
France
Contact: Ray Potts
Tel: +33 (0)4 6860 4890
Fax: +44 (0) 1432 880 191
Email: ray@pim-uk.com
Website: www.pim-uk.com
Sales territories: Middle East & the Indian Subcontinent
Specialisation: Trade, Education, Academic

A3.4 Indian Subcontinent

Aditya Books Pvt Ltd
119 Vinobha Puri
Lajpat Nagar - II
New Delhi 110 024
India
Tel: +91 98 1077 3223
Fax: +91 11 4172 4167
Email: sales@adityabooks.in
Website: www.adityabooks.in
Distributor
Sales territories: India, Bangladesh, & Sri
Lanka
Specialisation: STM, Law

Applied Media
206 Ashoka Apartment
Ranjeet Nagar Commercial Complex
Ranjeet Naga, New Delhi - 110 008
India
Contact: Sudhir Bansal
Tel: +91 11 570 7820
Fax: +91 11 2224 2778
Email: appliedmedia@vsnl.com
Sales territories: India

Book Bird
GPO Box 518
Mian Chambers, 3 Temple Road
Lahore
Pakistan
Contact: Mr Anwer Iqbal
Tel: +92 42 636 7275
Fax: +92 42 636 1370
Email: bookbird@brain.net.pk
Agent & distributor
Sales territories: Pakistan

Maya Publishers Pvt Ltd
4821 Parwana Bhawan (3rd Floor)
24 Ansari Road, Daryagan
New Dehli - 110 002
India
Contact: Surit Mitra
Tel:+91 11 6471 2521
Fax:+91 11 4354 9145
Email: surit@vsnl.com
Type: Publisher and distributor
Sales territories: India, Bangladesh, Nepal,
Bhutan, & Sri Lanka
Specialisation: Academic, general trade

Overleaf
P1/6 Ground Floor
D L F Phase 2
Gurgaon 122 002
India
Contact: Mr Seshadri
Tel: +91 124 256 7696
Fax: +91 11 2616 7249
Email: overleaf@vsnl.net
Sales territories: India, Nepal, Bangladesh,
& Sri Lanka
Specialisation: Academic, Education,
General Trade

Research Press
302A ABW Tower, IFFCO Crossing
MG Road, Gurgaon 122 001
Haryana
India
Contact: Ajay Parmar
Tel: + 91 124 404 0017
Email: aparmar@researchpress.co.in
Sales territories: India, Bangladesh, & Sri
Lanka
Specialisation: Academic, General Trade

Sara Books Pvt Ltd
G-1, Vardaan House
7/28 Ansari Road
Daryaganj
New Delhi 110 002
India
Contact: Ravindra Saxena
Tel: +91 11 2326 6107
Fax: +91 11 2326 6102
Email: ravindrasaxena@sarabooksindia.
com
*Sales territories: I*ndia, Bangladesh, & Sri
Lanka
Specialisation: Academic

Tahir M Lodhi Publishers'
Representatives
14-G Canalberg Multan Road
Lahore 53700
Pakistan
Tel: +92 42 543 7947
Fax: +92 42 543 7948
Email: tahirlodhi@gmail.com
Sales territory: Pakistan
Specialisation: Academic

Viva Books
4737/23 Ansari Road, Daryaganj
New Delhi – 110 002
India
Contact: Mr Vinod Vasishtha
Tel: +91 11 4224 2200
Fax: +91 11 4224 2240
Email: vinod@vivagroupindia.net
Sales territories: India
Specialisation: Academic, General Trade

A3.5 Far East

APAC Publishers Services PTE Ltd
31 Tannery Lane
#07-01 Dragon Land Building
Singapore 347788
Contact: Steven Goh
Tel: +65 6844 7333
Fax: +65 6747 8916
Email: service@apacmedia.com.sg
Sales territories: Singapore, Malaysia,
Thailand, Philippines, Hong Kong, China,
Indonesia, Brunei, Burma, Cambodia, &
Vietnam

Ashton International Marketing Services
PO Box 298, Sevenoaks
Kent TN13 1WU
UK
Contact: Julian Ashton
Tel:+44 (0) 1732 746093
Fax:+44 (0) 1732 746096
Email: jashton@ashtoninternational.com
Sales territories: Indonesia, Japan,
Malaysia, Philippines, Singapore, Taiwan,
& Thailand
Specialisation: Trade

Asia Publishers Services Limited
16/F Wing Fat Commercial Building
218 Aberdeen Main Road, Aberdeen
Hong Kong
Contact: Ed Summerson
Tel: +852 2553 9289
Fax: +852 2554 2912
Email: apshk@netvigator.com
Sales territories: Hong Kong, Taiwan,
China, Korea, & Philippines
Specialisation: College, Academic

Benji Ocampo Marketing Services for Publishers
57 STA Teresita, Kapitolyo
Metro Manila
The Philippines
Tel: +63 2 635 3592/3
Fax: +63 2 631 4470
Email: Benjie@compass.com.ph
Sales territories: Korea & Philippines
Specialisation: Academic, Trade

CKK Ltd.
8 Grove Road
Northwood
Middlesex HA6 2AP
UK
Contact: Theo Philips
Tel & Fax: +44 (0)1923 842499
Email: ckk.ltd@virgin.net
Sales territories: South-East Asia
Specialisation: Academic, Art

CRW Books
4 Topaz Road, Greenheights
Taytay, Rizal
The Philippines
Contact: Mr Tony Sagun
Tel: +63 2 660 5480
Fax: +63 2 660 0342
Email: lwwagent@compass.com.ph
Sales territories: Philippines
Specialisation: Trade

Delaney Global Publishers Services Inc
B 10 L 2 Maryland Homes 1
Landayan San Pedro
Laguna
The Philippines
Contact: Nanette Baremo
Tel: +63 2 869 34 52
Fax: +63 2 778 70 10
Email: dglopub@pldtvibe.net
Sales territories: Philippines & Guam

Ian Taylor Associates Ltd
12 Richborne Terrace
London SW8 1AU
UK
Tel: +44 (0) 20 7582 0071
Email: info@iantaylorassociates.com
Website: www.iantaylorassociates.com

Also at:

17C Unit 1
In Do Mansion
Hai Dian District
Beijing 100 098
China
Tel: +86 10 5873 2025
Fax: +86 10 5873 2015
Sales territory: China
Specialisation: Academic

Information & Culture Korea (ICK)

473-19 Seokyo-dong
Mapo-ku
Seoul 121-842
South Korea
Contact: Se-Yung Jun
Tel: +82 2 3141 4791
Fax: +82 2 3141 7733
Email: cs.ick@ick.co.kr
Sales territories: Korea
Specialisation: Academic

Publishers International Marketing

Timberham, 1 Monkton Close
Ferndown
Dorset BH22 9LL
Contact: Chris Ashdown
Tel: +44 (0)1202 896 210
Email: chris@pim-uk.com
Sales territories: North East & South East Asia
Specialisation: Trade

Sales East

43 Soi Pichit, Sukhumvit Road 18
Klong Toei
Bangkok 10110
Thailand
Contact: Peter Couzens
Tel: +66 2258 1305
Email: peter.couzens@saleseast.net
Sales territories: S.E. Asia
Specialisation: Trade

Transglobal Publishers Service Ltd

27-E Shield Industrial Centre
84/92 Chai Wan Kok Street
Tsuen Wan, New Territories
Hong Kong
Contact: Mr Anthony Choy
Tel: +852 2413 5322
Fax: +852 2413 7049
Email: info@transglobalpsl.com
Sales territories: Hong Kong & Macau
Specialisation: Education

United Publishers Services Limited

1-32-5 Higashi-shinagawa
Shinagawa-ku
Tokyo 140-0002
Japan
Contact: Mark Gresham
Tel: +81 3 5479 7251
Fax: +81 3 5479 7307
Email: info@ups.co.jp
Sales territories: Japan
Specialisation: Academic, Art, ELT, STM

Yasmy International Marketing

3-301 Park Ageo
3-1-48 Kashiwaza
Ageo 362-0075
Japan
Contact: Yasy Murayama
Tel: + 81 48 770 2003
Fax: + 81 48 770 2533
Email: yasy@yasmy.com
Sales territories: Japan & Korea

A3.6 Africa (sub-Sahara except South Africa)

A-Z Africa Book Services
105b Prins Muaritssingel
3043 PE Rotterdam
The Netherlands
Contact: Anita Zih
Tel: +31 10 415 4250
Fax: +31 10 415 1128
Email: anita.zih@planet.nl
Sales territories: Africa
Specialisation: Trade

Inter Media Africa Ltd
14 York Rise
London NW5 1ST
UK
Tel: +44 (0) 20 7267 8054
Fax: +44 (0) 20 7485 8462
Contact: Tony Moggach
Email: tony.moggach@tonymoggach.com
Sales territories: Africa
Specialisation: Trade

Kelvin van Hasselt Publishing Services
Willow House, The Street
Briningham, Norfolk
NR24 2PY
UK
Contact: Kelvin Van Hasselt
Tel: +44 (0)1263 862724
Fax: +44 (0)1263 862803
Email: kvhbooks@aol.com
Sales territories: Africa
Specialisation: Academic & Professional

Publishers International Marketing
Polfages
11420 Villautou
France
Contact: Ray Potts
Tel: +33 (0)4 6860 4890
Email: ray@pim-uk.com
Sales territories: Africa
Specialisation: Trade, Education, Academic

Richard Carman
16 Chapel Close
Comberbach, Northwich
Cheshire CW9 6BA
UK
Tel: +44 (0) 1606 891107
Fax: +44 (0) 1606 891107
Email: sales@richardcarman.co.uk
Sales territories: Africa (exc South Africa)
Specialisation: Academic/Trade

A3.7 Caribbean & South America

Vera Medeiros
Rua Dr. Esdras Pacheco Ferreira, 200
04507-060 - Vila Nova Conceição
São Paulo - SP - Brasil
Tel.:   + 55 11 3051- 2953
Mobile: +55 11 9553 -1100
Email: veralu.medeiros@uol.com.br
Sales territories: Argentina, Brazil
Specialisation: ELT, Academic

Humphrys Roberts Associates
5 Voluntary Place
Wanstead, London E11 2RP
UK
Contact: Chris Humphrys
Tel: +44 (0) 20 8530 5028
Fax: +44 (0) 20 8530 7870
Email: humph4HRA@gmail.com
Sales territories: Caribbean
Specialisation: Trade, Education

Also at:

Humphrys Roberts Associates
Caixa Postal 801
Ag. Jardim da Gloria
06709-970 Cotia SP
Brazil
Contact: Terry Roberts
Tel: +55 11 4702 4496 & 4702 6997
Fax: +55 11 4702 6896
Email: hrabrasil@uol.com.br
Sales territories: South America
Specialisation: Trade, Education

Also at:

Humphrys Roberts Associates
Avda Prol. San Carlos Pte.
M-1 L-45 C-4 Escalera 18, FRACC
Unidad San Carlos
Ecatepec 55027
Estado de Mexico
Contact: Sr Arturo Gutierrez Hernandez
Tel: +52 55 26 00 85 33
Fax: +52 55 26 00 88 80
Email: agutierrezh220795@hotmail.com
Sales territories: Central America
Specialisation: Trade, Education

InterMediaAmericana (IMA)
PO Box 8734
London SE21 7ZF
UK
Contact: David Williams
Tel: +44 (0) 20 7274 7113
Fax: +44 (0) 20 7274 7103
Email: sales@intermediaamericana.com
Sales territories: Caribbean & Latin
America
Specialisation: Trade

Kelvin van Hasselt Publishing Services
Willow House, The Street, Briningham
Norfolk NR24 2PY
UK
Contact: Kelvin Van Hasselt
Tel: +44 (0)1263 862724
Fax: +44 (0)1263 862803
Email: kvhbooks@aol.com
Sales territories: Caribbean
Specialisation: Academic & Professional

Appendix 4: Distributors in the major English language markets

The following is a selective listing of distributors in the major English language Commonwealth markets. For reasons of space, it is not fully comprehesive, it does not include details of the major publishing group such as Hachette, HarperCollins, Penguin, or Random House on the trade side or Elsevier, Macmillan, McGraw Hill, Oxford University Press, Pearson, Springer or Wiley, but gives the major companies dealing with small to medium sized UK publishers in their respective markets.

A4.1 Australia, New Zealand & Pacific Islands

Addenda Publishing Ltd
P O Box 78-224,
Level 1, 9 Rumuera Road, Newmarket
Auckland
New Zealand
Contact: Lea Greenstock
Tel: +64 9 529 9571
Fax: +64 9 529 9572
Email: addenda@addenda.co.nz
Website: www.addenda.co.nz
Sales territories: New Zealand
Specialisation: Trade fiction, Non-fiction, Children's

Capricorn Link (Australia) Pty. Ltd
2 Dowling Street, South Windsor
New South Wales SW 2756
Australia
Tel: +61 2 4560 1600
Fax: +61 2 4577 5288
Email: books@capricornlink.com.au
Website: www.capricornlink.com.au
Type: Distributor
Sales Territories: Australia
Specialisation: Trade

Cengage Learning
Level 7, 80 Dorcas Street
South Melbourne, Victoria 3205
Australia
Contact: Nicole McCarten
Tel: +61 3 9685 4111
Fax: +61 3 9685 4199
Email: nicole.mccarten@cengage.com
Website: www.cengage.edu.au
Sales territories: Australia
Specialisation: Education – Kindergarten to postgraduate, Library, Reference

DA Information Services Pty Ltd
648 Whitehorse Road, Mitcham
Victoria 3132
Australia
Tel: +61 3 9210 7777
Fax: +61 3 9210 7788
Email: publisherinfo@dadirect.com.au
Website: www.dadirect.com.au
Type: Distributor/Library Supplier
Sales territories: Australia, New Zealand and Papua New Guinea
Specialisation: Academic and Professional

David Bateman Ltd
Tarndale Grove
Albany Business Park, Bush Road
Auckland
New Zealand
Contact: Bryce Gibson
Tel: +64 9 415 7664
Fax: +64 9 415 8892
Email: bryceg@bateman.co.nz
Website: www.bateman.co.nz
Sales territories: Australia, New Zealand
and Papua New Guinea
Specialisation: Trade, Reference

DLS Australia (Pty) Ltd
12 Phoenix Court
Braeside, Victoria 3195
Australia
Tel: +61 3 9587 5044
Fax: +61 3 9587 5088
Email: books@dlsbooks.com
Website: www.dlsbooks.com
Sales territories: Australia, New Zealand
and Papua New Guinea
Specialisation: Library supplier and
distributor

Footprint Books Pty Ltd
1/6a Prosperity Parade
Warriewood
New South Wales 2102
Australia
Tel: +61 2 9997 3973
Fax: +61 2 9997 3185
Email: info@footprint.com.au
Website: www.footprint.com.au
Sales territories: Australia / New Zealand
Specialisation: Academic

Palgrave Macmillan
Postal Locked Bag 1
Prahan
Victoria 3181
Australia
Tel: +61 3 9825 1000
Fax: +61 3 9825 1010
Email: palgrave@macmillan.com.au
Website: www.palgravemacmillan.com.au
Sales territories: Australia
Specialisation: Academic

Peribo Pty Ltd
58 Beaumont Road, Mount Kuring-gai
New South Wales 2080
Australia
Tel: +61 2 9457 0011
Fax: +61 2 9457 0022
Email: info@peribo.com.au
Website: www.peribo.com.au
Sales territories: Australia, New Zealand,
Papua New Guinea
Specialisation: Trade

Rainbow Book Agencies Ltd
508 High Street, Preston
Victoria 3072
Australia
Tel: +61 3 9470 6611
Fax: +61 3 9470 2381
Email: rba@rainbowbooks.com.au
Website: www.rainbowbooks.com.au
Sales territories: Australia
Specialisation: Distributors to Religious
and Specialist Trade

The Scribo Group
Equinox Centre, 18 Rodborough Road
Frenchs Forest
New South Wales 2100
Australia
Contact: Chris Makin
Tel: +61 2 9975 5566
Fax: +61 2 9975 5599
Email: info@scribo.com.au
Web: www.scribo.com.au
Sales territories: Australia
Specialisation: Trade fiction, Non-Fiction
and Childrens

Southern Publishers Group
21 Newton Road
Auckland 1010
New Zealand
Contact: Charles Goulding
Tel: +64 9 360 0692
Fax: +64 9 360 0695
Email: hub@spg.co.nz
Website: www.spg.co.nz
Sales territories: New Zealand
Specialisation: Trade

University & Reference Publishers'
Services (UNIREPS)
UNSW Press
University of New South Wales
Sydney, New South Wales 2052
Australia
Tel: +61 2 9664 0906
Fax: +61 2 9664 5420
Email: info.press@unsw.edu.au
Website: www.unireps.com.au
Sales territories: Australia
Specialisation: Academic and
Professional, Non-Fiction, Education

Woodslane Pty. Ltd.
7/5 Vuko Place
Warriewood
New South Wales 2102
Australia
Contact: Andrew Guy
Tel: +61 2 9970 5111
Fax: +61 2 9970 5002
Email: info@woodslane.com.au
Website: www.woodslane.com.au
Sales territories: Australia, New Zealand
Specialisation: Business/Technology

A4.2 Canada

Codasat Canada Ltd
3122 Blenheim Street
Vancouver
British Columbia V6K 4J7
Canada
Contact: Sandra Hargreaves
Tel: +1 604 228 9952
Fax: +1 604 228 4733
Email: hargreaves@codasat.com
Website: www.codasat.com
Specialisation: Academic and Trade for
small to medium sized publishers.

Fitzhenry & Whiteside Limited
195 Allstate Parkway
Markham
Ontario L3R 4T8
Canada
Tel: +1 905 477 9700
Email: godwit@fitzhenry.ca
Website: www.fitzhenry.ca
Specialisation: General Trade

Georgetown Terminal Warehouses Limited
34 Armstrong Avenue
Georgetown
Ontario L7G 4R9
Canada
Tel: +1 905 873 2750
Fax: +1 905-873-6170
Email: info@gtwcanada.com
Website: www.gtwcanada.com
Specialisation: Academic & Trade

H B Fenn and Company Inc
34 Nixon Road
Bolton
Ontario L7E 1W2
Canada
Tel: +1 905 951 6600
Fax: +1 905 951 6601
Email: marnie.ferguson@hbfenn.com
Website: www.hbfenn.com
Specialisation: General Trade

McArthur & Co
322 King Street West, Suite 402
Toronto
Ontario M5V 1J2
Canada
Contact: Kim McArthur
Tel: +1 416 408 4007
Email: info@mcarthur-co.com
Website: www.mcarthur-co.com
Specialisation: General Trade

Raincoast Books
9050 Shaughnessy Street
Vancouver
BC V6P 6E5
Canada
Tel: +1 604 323 7100
Fax: +1 604 323 2600
Email: distribution@raincoast.com
Website: www.raincoast.com
Specialisation: General Trade

Renouf Publishing Company
Unit 1, 5369 Canotek Road
Ottawa
Ontario K1J 9J3
Canada
Contact: Gordon Grahame
Tel: +1 613 745 2665
Fax: +1 613 745 7660
Email: orders@renoufbooks.com
Website: www.renoufbooks.com
Specialisation:: Governmental, international business, health, environment and social sciences

Scholarly Book Services Inc
289 Bridgeland Ave, Unit 105
Toronto
Ontario M6A 1Z6
Canada
Tel: +1 416 504 6545
Fax: +1 416 504 0641
Email: customerservice@sbookscan.com
Website: www.sbookscan.com
*Specialisation:*Academic & literary trade r

UBC Press
University of British Columbia
2029 West Mall
Vancouver
British Columbia V6T 1Z2
Canada
Tel: +1 604 822 5959
Fax: +1 604 822 6083
Email: frontdesk@ubcpress.ca
Website: www.ubcpress.ubc.ca
Specialistion: Academic

UTP Distribution
5201 Dufferin Street
Toronto
Ontario M3H 5T8
Canada
Tel: +1 416 667 7791
Fax: +1 416 667 7832
Email: utpbooks@utpress.utoronto.ca
Website: www.utpress.utoronto.ca
*Specialisation:*Academic

Vanwell Distribution Services
1 Northrup Crescent
P 0 Box 2131, St Catharines
Ontario L2R 7S2
Canada
Tel: +1 905 937 3100
Fax: +1 905 937 1760
Email: sales@vanwell.com
Website: www.vanwell.com
*Specialisation:*Aviation, military & naval
books

A4.3 South Africa

Academic Marketing Services
PO Box 411738
Craighall Park 2024
South Africa
Contact: Michael Brightmore
Tel: +27 11 447 7441
Fax: +27 11 447 2314
Email: ams@icon.co.za
Specialisation: Academic
(Agent & Distributor)

Jacana Media
P.O. Box 291784, Melville 2109
South Africa
Contact: Shay Heydenrych
Tel: +27 11 628 3200
Fax: +27 11 482 7282
Email: shay@jacana.co.za
Website: www.jacana.co.za
Specialisation: General Trade

Peter Hyde Associates Pty Ltd
P 0 Box 2856, Cape Town 8000
South Africa
Contact; Peter Hyde
Tel: +27 21 447 5300
Fax: +27 21 447 1430
Email: peter@peterhyde.co.za
Specialisation: General Trade

Peter Matthews Agencies Ltd
18 Abel Moller Street, Brackenhurst
Alberton 1448
South Africa
Contact: Peter Matthews
Tel: +27 11 867 4175
Email: petermatthews@wol.co.za
Specialistion: General Trade

Phambili Books
PO Box 28680
Kensington 2101
South Africa
Contact: Maria Lastrucci
Tel: +27 11 455 3537
Fax: +27 11 455 3656
Email: phambili@wbs.co.za
Website: www.phambilibooks.co.za
Specialisation: General Trade

PSD Promotions (Pty) Ltd
30 Diesel Road
Isando 1600
South Africa
Contact: Lindsay Wagner
Tel: +27 11 392 6065
Fax: +27 11 392 6079
Email: lindsay@psdprom.co.za
Website: www.psdpromotions.co.za
Specialisation: General Trade

Real Books
P.O. Box 1040
Auckland Park 2006
South Africa
Tel: +27 11 403 3700
Fax: +27 11 339 3169
Email: info@realbooks.co.za
Specialisation: Trade and Educational

SG Distributors
P.O. Box 781021
Sadnton 2146
South Africa
Contact: Giulietta Campanelli
Tel: +27 11 444 9041
Fax: +27 11 444 9042
Email: giulietta@sgdistributors.co.za
Website: www.sgdistributors.co.za (under construction)
Specialisation: General Trade

Stephan Phillips (Pty) Ltd
3 Old Castle Brewery Building
6 Beach Road, Woodstock 7925
South Africa
Contact: George Thorne
Tel:+27 21 448 9839
Fax: +27 21 447 9879
Email: info@stephanphillips.com
Website: www.stephanphillips.com
Specialisation: General Trade

Trinity Books
P.O. Box 242, Randburg 2125
South Africa
Contact: Pat Wilmink
Tel: +27 11 787 4010
Fax: +27 11 787 8920
Email: trinity@iafrica.com
Specialisation: General Trade

Appendix 5: International sales agency checklist

Before choosing an international sales agency you should find out the follow:

Name of business and contact details:

Number of staff:

Territories covered:

Categories handled:

Lists current contracted:

Commission rates:

Promotion capacity and costs:

Typical commission rate and terms:

Travel/Schedule/typical call cycle for one year:

Do they have distribution capability, if so what are the terms for distribution (discounts,payment terms, returns facility):

Appendix 6   Driving international sales: a summary checklist

Here is quick summary and checklist of some of the elements that make up a successful international marketing effort.

Information: Providing regular feeds to the bibliographic databases of Nielsen Bookdata.

Distribution base: Preferably with a distributor who has a good export capacity.

Pricing: Be flexible in pricing and terms as appropriate to the markets.

Promotion (academic): Bookshop visits to major academic stores by representatives and mailing to department heads in relevant disciplines. Conference attendance is also important.

Promotion (trade): Establish your key accounts and work with them both directly and with your agents. Regular contact and visits will work in your favour.

Service: Providing a reliable sales service to agents, distributors and retailers is central to the success of any international sales effort.

Quality relationships in the market: This is a function of providing good service to customers, but it is essential to hold onto in regular direct meetings with key agents, library suppliers and retailers to build confidence and drive sales.

Inventory management: Accurate and timely deployment of stock is a crucial marketing skill as understocks or overstocks cost sales and profits. Inventory management is a key export marketing function and needs to be made the responsibility of someone in close touch with the markets.

Appendix 7: International and regional trade associations

Each of these trade associations have a link or contact details of their members (i.e., national trade associations) on their website.

7.1 IPA and regional publishers associations

International Publishers Association
3, avenue de Miremont, 1206 Geneva
Swizterland
Tel: 41 22 704 1820
Fax: 41 22 704 1821
skype: ipasecrariat
Email:

Asean Book Publishers Association
No 7-6, Block E2, Jalan P J U 1/42A
Dataran Prima, 47301 Petaling Jaya
Selangor Darul Enhsan
Malaysia
Tel:+ 603 7880 5840
Fax: + 603 7880 5841
Email: ariefhs@pts.com.my
Website: www.abpa.asia

African Publishers Network
2 Lynton Avenue, Marlborough
Harare
Zimbabwe
Tel/Fax: + 263 4 300790
Mobile: + 263 772 237572 / 773 446453
Email: mtainie@yahoo.com
or apnet@zol.co.zw
Website: www.african-publishers.net

Arab Publishers Association
2nd Floor, Sanndar Tower
92 Tahir Street, Dokki
Giza
Egypt
Tel: +202 37622058
Fax: +202 37622058 or 202 3748082
Email: nmahmoud@arab-pa.org
Website: www.arab-pa.org/En/
StaticPages/HomeEn.aspx

Asia-Pacific Publishers' Association (APPA)
c/o Korean Publishers Association
105-2, Sagan-dong, Jongno-gu, Seoul
110-190
Republic of Korea
Tel: +82 2 735 2702
Fax: +82 2 738 5414
Email: appa@kpa21.or.kr
Website: www.appa21.org

Caribbean Publishers Network
11 Cunningham Avenue
Kingston 6
Jamaica
Email: Capnet@colis.com
Website: www.capnetonline.net/

Federation of European Publishers (FEP)
Box 8, 31 rue Montoyer
1000 Bruxelles
Belgium
Tel: + 32 2 770 11 10
Fax: + 32 2 771 20 71
Email: info@fep-fee.eu
Website: www.fep-fee.be

Grupo Ibero-Americano de Editores (GIE)
Viamonte 1730, 1 Piso
1055 Buenos Aires
Argentina
Website: www.gieorg.org

Pan African Booksellers Association
Website: www.
panafricanbooksellersassociation.org/

Lily Nyariki
Chairperson PABA
Moi University Bookshop
P.O. Box 3900, Eldoret, Kenya
Tel: +254 53 43122 (Direct line) / +254 53
43259
Fax: +254 53 43259 / +254 53 43047
Mobile: +254 53 733 712117 / +254 53
720 777605
Email: lnyariki@yahoo.com / lnyariki@
multitechweb.com

7.2   International and regional bookseller associations

International Booksellers Federation
Rue de la Science 10
B-1000 Brussels
Website: www.ibf-booksellers.org/

European Booksellers Federation
Rue de la Science 10
B-1000 Brussels
Website: www.ebf-eu.org/

Appendix 8: List of major book fairs

See The Publishers Association's website (www.publishers.org.uk) for an up-to-date list of book fairs.

Abu Dhabi International Book Fair
P.O. Box 2380
Abu Dhabi
United Arab Emirates
Tel: +971 2 657 6180
Fax: +971) 2 444 5507
Email: info@adbookfair.com
Website: www.adbookfair.com

Baltic Book Fair
Kipsalas iela 8, Riga
LV-1048
Latvia
Tel: +371 6706 5023 / 6706 5000
Fax: +371 6706 5024 / 6706 5001
Email: bbf@bt1.lv
Website: www.bt1.lv

Beijing International Book Fair
16 Gongti East Road
Chaoyang District
Beijing 100020
China
Tel: +86 10 6586 6995
Fax: +86 10 6508 9188
Email: bibfmo@bibf.net
Website: www.bibf.net

Belgrade Book Fair
Bulevar vojvode Misica 14
11000 Belgrade
Serbia
Tel: +381 11 26 55 042
Fax: +381 11 26 55 042
Email: knjige@sajam.rs
Website: www.beogradskisajamknjiga.com

Bologna Children's Book Fair
Piazza Costituzione 6
40128 Bologna
Italy
Tel: +39 51 282 242 or 282 361
Fax: +39 51 637 4011
Email: bookfair@bolognafiere.it
Website: www.bookfair.bolognafiere.it

BookExpo America
383 Main Avenue
Norwalk, CT 06851
USA
Tel : +1-203 840 5507
Fax: +1-203 840 9507
Email: inquiry@bookexpoamerica.com
Website: www.bookexpoamerica.com

Book World Prague
Fügnerovo nám. 3
120 00 Praha 2
Czech Republic
Tel: +420 2 24 498 236
Fax: +420 2 24 498 754
Email: kalinova@svetknihy.cz
Website: www.bookworld.cz

Bucharest International Book Fair (BookFest)
Str. Dr. Iacob Felix 97, bl. 17A
sc. A, ap. 7, Sector 1
011035, Bucharest 1
Romania
Tel: +40 21 311 06 50
Fax: +40 21 311 59 41
Email: info@aer.ro
Website: www.bookfest.ro

Budapest International Book Festival
H-1367 Budapest
P.O.B. 130
Hungary
Tel: +36 1 34 32 537
Fax: +36 1 34 32 541
Email: festival@mkke.hu
Website: www.bookfestival.hu

Buenos Aires International Book Fair
Fundacion El Libro
Hipolito Yrigoyen 1628, 5, Second Floor
C1089AAF Buenos Aires
Republica Argentina
Tel: + 54 11 4370 0600
Fax: +54 11 4307 0607
Email: contacto@el-libro.org.ar
Website: www.el-libro.org.ar/internacional

Cairo International Book Fair
Corniche El Nil, Remlat Beulaq
Cairo
Egypt
Tel: +20 2 2577 5109
Fax: +20 2 2764 276
Email: info@Gebo.org.eg
Website: www.cairobookfair.org

Calcutta Book Fair
2B Jhama Pukur Lane, Kolkata 700 009
West Bengal, India
Tel: +91 33 2360 4588, 2354 4417
Fax: +91 33 2360 4566
Email: guild@cal2.vsnl.net.in
or pbguild@vsnl.net
Website: www.kolkatabookfaironline.com

Cape Town Book Fair
P.O. Box 51498, Waterfront, 8002
Cape Town
South Africa
Tel: +27 21 418 5493
Fax: +27 21 418 5949
Email: info@capetownbookfair.co.za
Website: www.capetownbookfair.com

Frankfurt Book Fair
Reineckstraße 3
60313 Frankfurt am Main
Germany
Tel: +49 69 2102 225
Fax: +49 69 2102 227
Email: info@book-fair.com
Website: www.book-fair.com

Gothenburg Book Fair
SE-412 94 Göteborg
Sweden
Tel: +46 (0) 31 708 84 00
Fax: +46 (0) 31 20 91 03
Email: info@goteborg-bookfair.com
Website: www.goteborg-bookfair.com

Guadalajara International Book Fair
Avenue Alemania 1370
Colonia Moderna
44190 Guadalajara, Jalisco
Mexico
Tel: +52 33 381 00 331
Fax: +52 33 326 80 921
Email: fil@fil.com.mx
Website: www.fil.com.mx

Liber International Book Fair
Parque Ferial Juan Carlos I
28042 Madrid
Spain
Tel: +34 91 722 5840
Fax: +34 91 722 5800
Email: liber@ifema.es
Website: www.liber.es

The London Book Fair
Gateway House, 28 The Quadrant
Richmond
Surrey TW9 1DN
UK
Tel: +44 (0)20 8271 2124
Fax: +44 (0)20 8334 0728
Email: lbf.helpline@reedexpo.co.uk
Website: www.londonbookfair.co.uk

Moscow International Book Fair
16 Malaya Dmitrovka St.
Moscow 127006
Russia
Tel: +7 495 699 4034
Fax: +7 495 973 2132, 299 8655
Email: mibf@mibf.ru
Website: www.mibf.ru

Moscow Non/Fiction Fair
"Expo-Park Exhibition Projects"
Central House , 10 Krimsky Val
Moscow 119049,
Russia
Tel: +7 495 657 9922
Fax: +7 499 238 4516
Website: www.moscowbookfair.ru

New Delhi Book Fair
5, Institutional Area
Vasant Kunj, Phase - II
New Delhi - 110070
India
Tel: +91 11 245 261 68
Email: nbtindia@ndb.vsnl.net.in
Website www.nbtindia.net.in

Riyadh International Book Fair
Tel: + 966 1 463 2830
Mobile: +966 1 5023 32266
Fax: +966 1 463 2830
Email: riyadhbookfair@moci.gov.sa
Website: www.riyadhbookfair.org.sa

Salon du Livre
52-54, quai de Dion-Bouton, CS 80001
92806 Puteaux Cedex
France
Tel: +33 1 47 56 64 31
Fax: +33 1 47 56 64 44
Email: info@reedexpo.fr
Website: www.salondulivreparis.com

Seoul International Book Fair
105-2, Sagan-dong, Jongno-gu
Seoul 110-190
South Korea
Tel: +82 2 738 5414
Fax: +82 2 738 5414
Email: kpa@kpa21.or.kr
Website: www.sibf.or.kr

St Petersburg International Book Fair
Lenexpo, Grand Ave VO, 103, Pav.6
199106 St. Petersburg
Russia
Tel: + 7 812 321 2867, 321 2747
Fax: + 7 812 321 2867, 321 2747
Email: E.Tsifirova@lenexpo.ru
Website: www.bookunion.spb.ru

Taipei International Book Fair
12F. No. 178, Section 1, Keelung Road
Taipei 110
Taiwan
Tel: + 886 2 2767 1268
Fax: + 886 2 2767 2808
Email: info@tibe.org.tw
Website: www.tibe.org.tw

Thessaloniki International Book Fair
Athanassiou Diakou Str. 4
117 42 Athens
Greece
Tel: +30 210 920 0327
Fax: +30 210 920 0305
Email: ezikou@ekebi.gr or
info@thessalonikibookfair.com
Website: www.thessalonikibookfair.com

Tokyo International Book Fair
18F Shinjuku-Nomura Bldg.,
1-26-2 Nishishinjuku
Shinjuku-ku, Tokyo 163-0570
Japan
Tel: +81 3 3349 8501
Fax: +81 3 3345 7929
Email: tibf-eng@reedexpo.co.jp
Website: www.tibf.jp

Turin International Book Fair
via Santa Teresa, 15
10121, Turin
IItaly
Tel: + 39 11 518 4268
Fax: + 39 11 561 2119
Email: info@fieralibro.it
Website: www.fieralibro.it

Warsaw International Book Fair
CHZ Ars Polona SA
03-933 Warszawa, ul. Obroncow 25
Poland
Tel: +48 22 509 8636
Fax +48 22 509 8610
Website: www.arspolona.com.pl
(NB: The 56th fair in 2011 was cancelled
due to a new fair organised by Murator
Expo S.A.

Appendix 9: Exporting booksellers, library suppliers, and wholesalers

This is a selective list for reasons of space, it is not fully comprehensive.

Askews and Holts Library Services Ltd.
218-222 North Road
Preston PR1 1SY
UK
Tel: +44 (0) 1772 298000
Fax: +44 (0) 1772 252358
Email: info@askewsandholts.com
Website: www. www.holtjackson.co.uk/

Bertrams
1 Broadland Business Park
Norwich, Norfolk, NR7 0WF
UK
Tel: +44 (0) 870 429 6665
Fax: +44 (0) 871 803 6709
Email: sales@bertrams.com
Website: www.bertrams.com

Blackwell Book Services
Beaver House, Hythe Bridge Street
Oxford, OX1 2ET
UK
Tel: +44 (0)1865 333 000
Email: sales@blackwell.co.uk
Website: www.blackwell.co.uk/
libraryservices

Coutts Information Services Ltd.
Avon House, Headlands Business Park
Ringwood, Hampshire BH24 3PB
UK
Tel: + 44 (0)1425 471160
Fax: + 44 (0)1425 471525
Website: www.couttsinfo.com/

Dawson Books
Foxhills House, Brindley Close
Rushden, Northamptonshire NN10 6DB
UK
Tel: +44 (0)1933 417500
Fax: +44 (0)1933 417501
Website: www.dawsonbooks.co.uk/

Gardners Books
1 Whittle Drive, Eastbourne
East Sussex, BN23 6QH
UK
Tel: +44 (0)1323 521777
Customer Care Fax: +44 (0)1323 521666
Email: export@gardners.com
Website: www.gardners.com

Mallory International
Aylesbeare Common
Business Park, Exmouth Road
Aylesbeare, Devon EX5 2DG
UK
Tel: +44 (0) 1395 239199
Fax: +44 (0) 1395 239168
Email: enquiries@malloryint.co.uk
Website: www.malloryint.co.uk

Starkmann Ltd
6 Broadley Street, London NW8 8AE
UK
Tel: +44 (0) 20 77245335
Fax: +44 (0) 20 7724 9863
Email: orders@starkmann.co.uk
Website: www.starkmann.com

The Book Depository
Goodridge Training Estate
Goodrige Avenue
Quedederley
Gloucestershire G12 2EB
Contact: Steve Potter
Tel: +44 (0) 1453 307905
Email Steve@bookdepository.co.uk
Web: www.bookdepository.com

Appendix 10: List of freight forwarders

The following is a selective list of freight forwarders. For reasons of space, it is not fully comprehensive.

C.T Freight (UK)) LTD
Unit D, Northumberland Close
Stanwell, Middlesex TW19 7LN
UK
Contact: Terry Croft, International Sales & Development
Tel: +44 (0) 1784 245 777
Fax: +44 (0) 1784 245 888
Email: terry@ctfreight.co.uk
Website: www.ctfreight.co.uk/

F.J.T. Logistics Ltd
Unit B1, Hubert Road
Brentwood, Essex CM14 4RF
UK
Contact: Ray Harper, Director
Tel: +44 (0)1277 215 600
Fax: +44 (0)1277 260237
Email: ray@fjtit.com
Website: www.fjtlogistics.com/

OHL Global Freight Management and Logistics (formerly Activair)
Unit 1 Action Court
Ashford Road, Ashford
Middlesex TW15 1XS
UK
Contact: Paul Barrett, Sales Director
Tel: +44 (0) 1784 890005
Fax: +44 (0) 1784 890011
Website: www.activair.ohl.com

OHL Global Freight Management and Logistics (formerly Activsea)
ActivHouse, Watkins Close
Burnt Mills Industrial Estate
Basildon, Essex SS13 1TL
UK
Contact: Martin Caines, General Manager
Tel: +44 (0) 1268 724 400
Email: sales@ohl.com
Website: www.ohl.com

The PSL Group Ltd
Quayside Park, Bates Road
Maldon, Essex CM9 5FA
UK
Contact: Rob Millin, Manager
Tel: +44 (0) 1621 854 451
Fax: +44 (0) 01621 843 639
Email: european@pslgroup.net
Website: www.pslgroup.net

SBS Worldwide Ltd (Sea)
SBS Cargo Centre
Anchor Boulevard
Crossways, Dartford DA2 6SB
UK
Contact: Steve Walker
Tel: +44 (0)1322 424 700
Fax: +44 (0)1322 285 591
Email: ocean@sbsworldwide.com
Website: www.sbsworldwide.com

SBS Worldwide Ltd (Air)
SBS House, Blackthorne Road
Colnbrook
SL3 0SB
UK
Tel: +44 (0)1753 210 100
Fax: +44 (0)1753 681 581
Email: air@sbsworldwide.com
Website: www.sbsworldwide.com

Trans Global Freight Management Ltd
Woodlands, 79 High Street
Greenhithe, Kent DA9 9RD
UK
Contact: Charles J Hurst
Export Sales Manager
Tel: +44 (0) 8453 376500
Fax: +44 (0) 8453 376550
Email: greenhithe@tgfml.com
Website: www.tgfml.com

Appendix 11: UK Trade and Investment support opportunities

Whether you are venturing into selling overseas for the first time, or you are an experienced exporter trying to break into new markets, UKTI offers a range of trade support services to help you.

- If you are a new exporter, representatives at your regional UKTI office can help you prepare for trading overseas through an assessment and skills based programme.

- They can also help with stand costs by providing financial support to eligible Small and Medium Sized Enterprises (SMEs) as part of their **Tradeshow Access Programme (TAP)**. The levels of grants vary from £1,000 - £1,800. The Publishers Association is the UKTI Accredited Trade Organisation (ATO) who administers this scheme for the publishing industry and full details are available on the PA's website (www.publishers.org.uk).

- They offer two key research and contact services, **Overseas Market Introduction Service (OMIS)** and **Export Marketing Research Scheme (EMRS)**. OMIS can provide help at any stage - from initial research, to arranging a market visit, to using their contacts and facilities to help close a major deal. While EMRS, administered by the British Chambers of Commerce, can provide grants of up to 50 per cent of the agreed costs of marketing research projects to eligible companies.

UKTI have also developed an online marketing toolkit, which is free to access at www.creative-industries.co.uk. It contains creative industry sector marketing messages and supporting facts and figures that you can use in your international marketing and PR campaigns.

For details of your local adviser, enter your postcode in the Local Office Database on the UKTI website: www.ukti.gov.uk. Alternatively, call the UKTI Equity Service on +44 (0)20 7215 8000. The devolved administrations in Scotland, Wales and Northern Ireland have their own arrangements for local delivery services.

Appendix 12: The Publishers Association and other useful contacts

12.1 The Publishers Association

The Publishers Association
29B Montague Street
London WC1B 5BW
UK
Tel: +44 (0) 20 7691 9191
Fax: +44 (0) 20 7691 9199
Email: mail@publishers.org.uk
Website: www. publishers.org.uk

The PA offers a number of tools to its members to assist with implementing their export strategy:

- The PA's website contains a wealth of information including our unique PA Market Reports; fully comprehensive overviews of a wide range of export markets, free for download for our members and available for a small fee for non-members.

- The PA's International Book Fairs division offers a full service to assist you with exhibiting at major book fairs either on your own stand or as part of a collective. Our presence is often accompanied by networking events for our exhibitors.

- The PA has a long tradition of organising trade delegations to emerging markets, especially to China. In 2010 the delegations went to India and Russia and more delegations are planned for 2011 and beyond (see our website for details).

- The PA has an International Board whose members look at how we can work on collective basis to address issues concerning the export market such as piracy and market access. A subset of Working Parties looks at territory specific issues across Europe, Asia, Africa, Latin America, Middle East and the Caribbean such as marketing the English Language and British Books.

A major outcome of the Board and working parties is the annual PA International Conference, providing a day packed with presentations and dialogues about export markets and factors affecting the export business.

- The PA has published two other guides to help exporters:

PA Guide to International Book Fairs
(Gloria Bailey, Peter Newsom & Lynette Owen, 2010)

PA Guide to Aid-Funded Markets
(Chris Nott & Kern Roberts, 2010)

In addition, the PA has published a manual on how to go digital:

PA Guide toGoing Digital
(Linda Bennett, 2010)

Finally, we cannot mention export without mentioning UK Trade & Investment (UKTI). The PA is the only UKTI Accredited Trade Organisation for the publishing industry. We administer the Tradeshow Access Programme grants for exhibiting at book fairs, and manage sector funding which traditionally contributes towards networking events and supports the PA International Conference. We are extremely grateful to them for this invaluable financial support on offer to publishers who qualify. UKTI also offers a suite of services which provide tailored solutions to publishers with export needs with excellent outcomes.

For further information visit the PA's website: www.publishers.org.uk

12.2   Other useful contacts

Exports Credit Guarantee Department
PO Box 2200, 2 Exchange Tower
Harbour Exchange Square
London E14 9GS
UK
Tel: +44 (0)20 7512 7000
Fax: +44 (0)20 7512 7649
Website: www.ecgd.gov.uk

HM Revenue & Customs (statistics)
3rd Floor Central, Alexander House
21 Victoria Avenue, Southend on Sea
Essex SS99 1AA
UK
Tel: +44 (0) 1702 367 485
Email: uktradeinfo@hmrc.gsi.gov.uk
Website:www.uktradeinfo.com

Independent Publishers Guild
PO Box 12, Llain
Login SA34 0WU
Wales
UK
Tel: +44 (0) 1437 563335
Fax: +44 (0)1437 562071
Email: info@ipg.uk.com
Website: www.ipg.uk.com

Institute of Export
Export House, Minerva Business Park
Lynch Wood, Peterborough
Cambridgeshire PE2 6FT
UK
Tel: +44 (0)1733 404400
Fax: +44 (0)1733 404444
Website: www.export.org.uk

Publishing Scotland
Scottish Book Centre, 137 Dundee Street,
Edinburgh, EH11 1BG
Scotland
UK
Tel: +44 (0) 131 228 6866
Fax: +44 (0) 131 228 3220
Email: enquiries@publishingscotland.org
Website: www.publishingscotland.co.uk

UK Trade and Investment
Kingsgate House, 66-74 Victoria Street
London SW1E 6SW
UK
Tel: +44 (0) 207 215 8000
Website: www.ukti.gov.uk/

*Since 2010, publishing is under the remit
of UKTI's Education & Skills, Publishing,
Experience and Attractions Sector Team.
Education & Skills Sector Officer: Euan
Scott
Tel: +44 (0)20 7215 4283
Email: euan.scott@uktradeinvest.gov.uk*

**UKTI's Export Marketing Research
Scheme**
British Chambers of Commerce
The British Chambers of Commerce
Oak Tree Court, Binley Business Park
Harry Weston Road
Coventry CV3 2UN
UK
Tel: +44 (0) 24 7669 4484
Fax: +44 (0) 24 7669 5844
Email: emr@britishchambers.org.uk
Website: www.britishchambers.org.uk

Lightning Source UK Ltd.
Milton Keynes UK

174005UK00001B/22/P